Small Projects . . .

Nigel Ostime

RIBA  **Publishing**

Small Projects Handbook

© RIBA Enterprises Ltd, 2014, reprinted 2017

Revised to include CDM 2015 Regulations

Published by RIBA Publishing, part of RIBA Enterprises Ltd, The Old Post Office, St Nicholas Street, Newcastle upon Tyne, NE1 1RH

ISBN 978 1 85946 549 3
Stock code 82649

The right of Nigel Ostime to be identified as the Author of this Work has been asserted in accordance with the Copyright, Designs and Patents Act 1988 sections 77 and 78.

British Library Cataloguing-in-Publication Data

A catalogue record for this book is available from the British Library.

Publisher: Steven Cross
Commissioning Editor: Sarah Busby
Project Editor: Richard Blackburn
Designed & Typeset by Kneath Associates
Printed and bound by W&G Baird Ltd in Great Britain

While every effort has been made to check the accuracy and quality of the information given in this publication, neither the Author nor the Publisher accept any responsibility for the subsequent use of this information, for any errors or omissions that it may contain, or for any misunderstandings arising from it.

RIBA Publishing is part of RIBA Enterprises Ltd.
www.ribaenterprises.com

Foreword

About half of practices in the UK have between one and five people and a further quarter have five to ten, with an average turnover per fee earner of around £55,000pa. This indicates that each fee earner is typically working on around £1m of construction activity each year - the amount identified as representing the upper limit for small projects in this book.

For over fifty years architects seeking project management advice have been able to refer to the *RIBA Job Book*, which contains guidance intended to cover all project sizes, up to multi-million pound, complex developments. Small projects however have their own, particular requirements that can be quite different in nature and process. Up to now, the RIBA has not published advice specifically targeted towards that significant majority of the profession who make a living from the <£1m projects. This book bridges that gap.

The elephant in the room for small practices has long been the difficulty they face trying to make a reasonable income that reflects the time it takes to qualify, let alone the years of experience needed to practice with confidence. This book aims to help in this regard – to make your practice and project management processes more efficient whilst maintaining the quality that will help to bring in the next job.

I commend this book for its clarity and direct, hands-on approach and feel sure it will help you to increase turnover and profit whilst providing value to your clients.

Stephen R Hodder MBE
President RIBA 2013-15

Contents

Introduction

The purpose of this book is to provide a hands-on guide to running small projects aimed at practising architects, Part 3 students, technologists and other building and interior designers. A small project is defined here as being up to £1m construction value but there is another threshold of up to £250,000 that is common amongst the case studies. The key difference between these two will be the form of construction contract used and this matter is covered in the chapters on Procurement and Stage 5: Construction. The advice given in this book is applicable to a broad range of projects with varying construction value as well as a range of practice sizes and building sectors.

The Small Projects Handbook draws on content from both the *RIBA Job Book, 9th edition* and the *Handbook of Practice Management, 9th edition*, but it aims to provide smaller practices and those taking on smaller architectural projects with an alternative guide to those publications that meets their distinct needs. It takes a different approach in style, offering a more accessible, friendly, small-scale tone, broken up with case material illustrating problems and solutions and quotes from small practices to root it in real practice. There are sample letters and forms covering key issues and web-based accompaniments including the action checklists, standard letters, forms and spreadsheets that can be downloaded free-of-charge and adapted for a specific project.

The book gives comprehensive but succinct step-by-step guidance on best practice in managing small projects aligned to the RIBA Plan of Work 2013. It also includes advice on project-related practice management, marketing and so on, but without any 'fat' focusing on distinctly practical matters and effective, efficient working practices.

It can be difficult to maintain a business based on small projects and this book aims to help practitioners tighten up their project processes whilst ensuring they perform well and get the next commission or a referral.

It focuses on concerns such as making a profit from small-margin projects, as well as efficiency, outsourcing, collaboration, multi-skilling, self-management, cash flow and so on.

The book gives practical advice on how to manage the work, giving confidence to practitioners that if they follow the advice they will have done a good job, made a profit and get repeat business.

Structure of the book

Set out in four sections against the RIBA Plan of Work 2013 work stages, the book guides the reader through all the essential elements of running a successful project:

Section I	Cradle to Cradle
Stage 7	In Use
Stage 0	Strategic Definition
Stage 1	Preparation & Brief

Section II	Progressive Fixity
Stage 2	Concept Design
Stage 3	Developed Design

Section III	Preparing to Build
Stage 4	Technical Design
Procurement	

Section IV	On Site
Stage 5	Construction
Stage 6	Handover & Close Out

The grouping of stages into sections reflects the fact that for small projects some activities can be amalgamated and this is often reflected in the appointment and Project Programme. Each stage is however given its own chapter in the book.

Stage 7 has been grouped with Stages 0 and 1, reflecting the cyclical nature of the Plan of Work 2013 and the opportunity for passing learning from one project to the next.

While Procurement (of the contractor) is a flexible task bar in the Plan of Work 2013, it has been set out as a stage following development of the Technical Design during Stage 4 as this is most frequently the case for small projects. These activities can however take place from Stage 2 onwards if appropriate.

Each stage is set out in the same way, recognising the iterative nature of the project process:

Introduction
Plan of Work 2013
Project activities
Information required
Stage activities
Information exchange
Sustainability checkpoints
Case study
Project issues
Case study
Practice issues
Stage summary

The case studies incorporate images, drawings and quotes from practices illustrating real-life project issues.

There is a list of references to other useful books and websites at the end of the book.

The project activities are presented as a series of checklists that cover the key actions in each stage. These can be used as an editable project plan and can be downloaded for free at www.ribabookshops.com/SPH.

It should be noted that while the activities are broadly set out in chronological order, it is important to assimilate all the advice in a single stage before commencing work, as some activities will occur in a different order in different projects.

Following the project activities are 'project issues', giving advice on a range of project-related topics and standard letters, forms, spreadsheets and so on.

At the end of each chapter are 'practice issues'. Although not necessarily related to a specific project stage, these are set out where they were considered to be most pertinent, with cross-referencing in other parts of the book to aid navigation. The features covered include:

Office management
Financial management
Risk management
People management
IT management, plus CAD and BIM for small practices
Knowledge management
Marketing and business development

Icons identify different types of advice:

Tips

Tools of the trade

Watchpoints

BIM-related matters

Terminology

This book follows the terminology used in the Plan of Work 2013, which can be found at www.ribaplanofwork.com. Plan of Work terms are capitalised in the text and a glossary is included at the end of the book.

Small practices are defined by the RIBA as:

Micro practices:	1–5 people
Small practices:	5–10 people
Small-medium practices:	10–20 people

This book covers projects that all of the above are likely to deal with and uses the term 'small practice' to cover all firms up to 20 people in size. Indeed it is likely that some large-to-medium-sized practices (20–50 people) will also undertake the sort of work this book covers.

How to use this book

The book has been designed to be followed iteratively, stage by stage, as the project progresses. When the action checklists are downloaded electronically to make a job-specific project plan, notes can be added both to plan future activities and as a record of when specific tasks have been completed.

The book can also be used as a reference source for the various pieces of advice it contains on project and practice management and the sources of further reading.

The standard letters set out in this book are also downloadable from the website. Writing style can vary with the individual so you are of course free to adapt them as you see fit, but take care not to eliminate any matters that are critical from a legal point of view. Always take advice when you are not certain of the correct way to deal with a particular issue. The letters are not intended to be comprehensive in their scope but cover key matters at each stage of a project.

Nigel Ostime

About the author

Nigel Ostime is an architect with over 25 years' experience during which he has been responsible for projects in a wide range of sectors including offices, residential, retail, town centre mixed-use and industrial/distribution buildings. He has delivered planning permissions on sensitive sites, both urban and rural, and has expertise in the management and coordination of multidisciplinary consultant teams through all project stages.

He is currently Project Delivery Director at Hawkins\Brown, an internationally-renowned, award winning practice of architects, interior designers, urban designers and researchers.

Nigel is an active member of the RIBA, being a member of the Practice and Profession Committee and chair of the Client Liaison Group, which provides an interface between the Institute and client bodies. He also sits on the H&S Steering Group and set up the Future Leaders initiative, an education programme for business-focused, post-Part 3 skills for architects.

He has edited the last two editions of both the RIBA Job Book (2008 and 2013) and the Handbook of Practice Management (2010 and 2013) and is author of the RIBA Client's Guide to Engaging an Architect, Commercial and Domestic versions (2017).

He lives in North London with his wife, three children and six bicycles.

Acknowledgements

The author would like to thank Adrian Dobson and Dale Sinclair for their input and advice on the book generally. Thanks also to Richard Fairhead and Martin Coyne for their advice on BIM and IT; to Luke Davies for advice on planning; to James Ritchie on health and safety; to Koko Udom on the new RIBA construction contracts; to Bill Gething for developing the original Sustainability Checkpoints and to Gary Clark and BSRIA for the information on Soft Landings. Thanks to James Hutchinson for his help in sourcing the case studies and liaising with the practices concerned, and a particular thanks to the many small practices who have contributed some brilliant and intricately conceived projects. They are a testament to what can be achieved on a small budget by designers who care enough to deliver more than the client had thought possible. Finally thanks to Sarah Busby, who has helped enormously in shaping the book, giving sound advice on its content, format and design.

CDM Regulations 2015

The CDM Regulations 2015 were being drafted when the first print of this book was published but this reprint has provided the opportunity to bring it up-to-date. References to CDM coordinators have been omitted and the new role of principal designer has been incorporated into the stage activities and the supporting material. This role has provided new opportunities for architects who are, on the whole, ideally placed to perform the new functions. It is a separate role to that of architect/designer and should be the subject of a separate appointment as it will have different terms and potentially a different time frame.

The activities of the principal designer have not been added to the action checklists as there is some very comprehensive reference material that has been published on the subject and this is noted in the revised 'Further reading' section at the back of the book. The activities do however note where the architect/designer interfaces with the principal designer role, in a similar way to the previous interface with the CDMC.

It is important that designers take on the role of principal designer in the spirit of the legislation. It is not unduly demanding and will undoubtedly result in better outcomes with regard to health and safety of workers on site and users and maintainers of the finished buildings.

The Construction (Design and Management) Regulations 2015 are the main set of regulations for managing health, safety and welfare on construction projects. CDM applies to all building and construction work and includes new build, demolition, refurbishment, extensions, repair and maintenance.

There are three key duty holders under the regulations: the client, the principal designer and the principal contractor. The principal designer is the designer who has control over the pre-construction phase of the project. The role is performed by a company or individual who has appropriate 'skills, knowledge and experience' relevant to the project, to enable them to manage and coordinate the pre-construction phase, including any design work carried out after construction begins. The principal designer needs to have the organisational capacity to carry out the role and be able to work collaboratively with the client, other designers and the principal contractor.

The principal designer must be appointed by the client in writing and – where there is a requirement for a principal designer - until this has happened, the role defaults to the client themselves. If the work is to be undertaken by a single contractor there is no requirement for the client to appoint a principal designer or a principal contractor.

RIBA Plan of Work 2013

The RIBA Plan of Work 2013 was published in May 2013 with the intention of consolidating recent developments in sustainable design and BIM processes as well as regularising the complexities of the different forms of procurement and encouraging collaborative project processes. It is now the standard tool for managing construction projects in the UK.

The key changes it brings are:

A matrix of:

    8 numbered stages (0–7) rather than 11 lettered ones (A–L)

    8 task bars to cover the key project activities

Flexible task bars for the '3 Ps': Procurement, (Project) Programming and (Town) Planning, which allows the Plan of Work 2013 to adapt to multiple project formats

Sustainability Checkpoints added

Common defined terms introduced

It has also defined 'Project Objectives', which are to be set out in the Initial Project Brief, and 'Project Strategies', which are developed during Stages 2 and 3 to be absorbed into Stage 4 outputs. Refer to the RIBA Plan of Work glossary at the end of the book for an explanation of these and how they fit into the project process.

The customisable format of the RIBA Plan of Work 2013 is as relevant to small practices as to large ones, and it is important that the domestic construction industry adopts common terminology and processes to help drive efficiency.

Small projects play just as important a part as large, multi-million pound developments in creating a better built environment and building the UK economy. Universal uptake of the new version of the Plan of Work is vital if building designers are to play their part in transforming and modernising the UK construction industry into a unified, collaborative supply chain.

Go to www.ribaplanofwork.com for further information and to download a free, customisable Plan of Work to use on your next project.

The RIBA has published a Small Projects Plan of Work which can be found at https://www.architecture.com/RIBA/Professionalsupport/RibaPlanOfWork.aspx. There is a copy of this on pages 14-15.

RIBA
Plan of Work

Small Project Plan of Work

The RIBA Plan of Work organises the process of briefing, designing, constructing, maintaining, operating and using building projects into 8 stages.

The RIBA Small Project Plan of Work has been published to enable closer working between clients and architects and to suggest the key tasks for small projects. It should be used in conjunction with the RIBA Plan of Work 2013 to organise project tasks, as many tasks are left out of this document to keep it as simple as possible.

The **Sustainability Checkpoints**, that provide sustainable design tasks relevant at all project scales, and further information on **Project Strategies** can be found at www.ribaplanofwork.com.

The RIBA Plan of Work 2013 should be used solely as guidance for the preparation of detailed professional services contracts and building contracts.

▶Stages Tasks▼	0 Strategic Definition	1 Preparation and Brief	2 Concept Design
Core Objectives	Identify client's **Business Case** and **Strategic Brief** and other core project requirements. *[Sustainability Checkpoint – 0]*	Develop **Project Objectives**, **Project Outcomes**, **Sustainability Aspirations**, **Project Budget**, other parameters or constraints and develop **Initial Project Brief**. Undertake **Feasibility Studies** and review of **Site Information**. *[Sustainability Checkpoint – 1]*	Prepare Concept Design, including outline proposals for structural design, building services systems, outline specifications and preliminary **Cost Information** along with relevant **Project Strategies** in accordance with **Design Programme**. Agree alterations to brief and issue **Final Project Brief**. *[Sustainability Checkpoint – 2]*
Procurement Professional services and building contracts based on a traditional procurement route	Initial considerations for assembling the project team.	Agree **Schedule of Services**. Appoint design team including **Principal Designer**.	
Planning Consent, Building Regulations and Health and Safety (CDM) Overview of regulatory requirements.		Conduct initial pre-**Planning** application discussions. *[if required to determine the suitability of **Feasibility Studies**].* inform **Client** of their regulatory responsibilities including **Health and Safety**.	Collate **Pre-Construction Information**. Conduct pre-**Planning** application discussions. Submit outline planning applications. *[Detailed planning applications should be made only where to meet specific client need, the associated risks should be included in the Stage sign-off].*
Information Exchanges Generally at stage completion	Strategic Brief.	Initial Project Brief.	Concept Design including outline structural and building services design, preliminary **Cost Information** and **Final Project Brief**.
Level of Detail Suggested level of detail for design and level of information for specification *[If using BIM the model will be a deliverable.]*			1:1250 Location Plan. 1:500 Site Plan. 1:100 Plans, Sections and Elevations.

© RIBA 2016

RIBA
Architecture.com

3 Developed Design	**4** Technical Design	**5** Construction	**6** Handover and Closeout	**7** In Use
Prepare Developed Design, including coordinated and updated proposals for structural design, building services systems, outline specifications, **Cost Information** and **Project Strategies** in accordance with **Design Programme**. *[Sustainability Checkpoint – 3]*	Prepare Technical Design in accordance with **Project Strategies** to include all architectural, structural and building services information, specialist subcontractor design and specifications, in accordance with **Design Programme**. *[Sustainability Checkpoint – 4]*	Offsite manufacturing and onsite Construction in accordance with the **Construction Programme** and resolution of **Design Queries** from site as they arise. *[Sustainability Checkpoint – 5]*	Handover of building and conclusion of **Building Contract**. *[Sustainability Checkpoint – 6]*	Undertake In Use services in accordance with **Schedule of Services**. *[Sustainability Checkpoint – 7]*
	Issue **Technical Design** for tender. Tenders assessed and **Building Contract** awarded including appointing **Principal Contractor**. Specialist sub-contractor Stage 4 information reviewed post award.	Administer **Building Contract** to **Practical Completion**, including regular site inspections and review of progress.	Conclude administration of **Building Contract**.	Maintain relationship with Client, offer additional In Use services as appointed.
Submit **Planning** application. Undertake third party consultations as required. *[Detailed planning applications should only be made prior to the design coordination activities if approved by the client. The design coordination activities should be concluded prior to stage 3 completion].*	Review **Planning Conditions** following granting of consent. Discharge pre-Construction **Planning Conditions** as required and others where possible. Prepare and submit **Building Regulations** submission and any other third party submissions requiring consent.	Collate **Health and Safety File**. **Contractor** to comply with any construction-specific **Planning Conditions**.	Comply with pre-occupancy **Planning Conditions**. Advise **Client** of need to comply with in-use **Planning Conditions**.	
Developed Design, including the coordinated architectural, structural and building services design and updated **Cost Information**.	Completed Technical Design of the project.		'As-constructed' Information including **Health and Safety File** *[at begining of stage]*. **Feedback** reports.	
1:1250 Location Plan. 1:500 Site Plan. 1:100 Plans, Sections and Elevations. 1:50 Sketch Details. Outline **Specification**.	1:500 Block Plan. 1:100 Site plan including drainage, external works, etc. 1:50 Plans, Sections and Elevations. 1:20 Detailed plans and sections. 1:10/1:5/Full Size component details Door/Window/Finishes and other Schedules. Detailed **Specification**.		1:100 Site plan including drainage, external works, etc. 1:50 Plans, Sections and Elevations. Detailed Specification. Structural, building services and specialist subcontractor information *[as appropriate if not incorporated onto the architects information]*.	

Section I

Cradle to Cradle

Introduction

This book is laid out according to the RIBA Plan of Work 2013, which has been designed to be flexible for all project types and all forms of procurement, including small projects. The Plan of Work comprises two new stages, one being Stage 7: In Use, which covers activities occurring after completion of defects work, and relates to how the building is operated and maintained throughout its life.

So why does the book start at the end?

The Plan of Work 2013 is cyclical in nature, recognising the importance of Post-occupancy Evaluation (POE) and the benefits of maintaining a good working relationship with the client – and through them to other potential clients. On average two-fifths of a practice's work comes from repeat business. This rises to three-fifths for large-to-medium-sized practices, dropping to one-third for micro practices, but still significant nonetheless. It is therefore an important part of business development but also, potentially, a new source of fee income if the project team can take on facilities management activities. For small projects, where post-completion activities are less likely, referrals are the most likely outcome, but still well worth pursuing.

Stage 0, the other new stage in the Plan of Work 2013, follows on from Stage 7 by way of learning from past experience to improve the next job. In order to drive efficiency – a key theme of this book – it is critical that this is optimised so that the designer is not reinventing the wheel each time a new project is undertaken. Stage 0 is the point at which the first stage of the briefing process commences – preparation of the Strategic Brief. Strategic considerations might include considering different sites, and whether to extend, refurbish or build new. They might also include the key Project Outcomes (a mixture of subjective and objective criteria), the likely composition of the project team and the overall Project Programme.

Finally there is Stage 1, which includes developing the Initial Project Brief and any related Feasibility Studies. This stage of the briefing process involves more detailed discussions with the client to ascertain the Project Objectives, the client's Business Case (if applicable) and conclusions from the Feasibility Studies. It is critical that design activities are not commenced before the necessary information has been gathered on the site constraints (and the opportunities offered) and the designer has a full understanding of the building type, best practice in relation to that building sector, benchmark projects, relevant regulations and the planning context.

The initial Feasibility Studies will be undertaken simultaneously with the brief development but these studies should not go into too much detail – they are strategic studies undertaken to inform the brief and no more than that.

The necessary office systems should be in place and implemented from the outset. See the advice set out under Stage 0: Setting up an efficient practice.

Also of importance is having an appointment for the services to be delivered that is fully understood and agreed by the client. This should include a detailed breakdown of activities and deliverables, set out against the Project Programme.

Stages 7, 0 and 1 have been grouped together to form the first section of the book, reflecting the fact that:

— All projects should build on knowledge gained from previous experience which feeds into the briefing process.
— Stages 0 and 1 are where the project is set up and the necessary knowledge gathered to ensure a comprehensive optioneering process.

If the project gets off to a good start it has every chance of being successful, profitable and leading to subsequent commissions. The corollary to this is a project started before the necessary preparation has taken place, which will always be difficult to bring back on track. Preparation is everything.

> **Key advice for these stages**

Take time to get the project started properly, with a considered brief and knowledge of the site and building type before design commences. It will be time well spent that adds value to the end product.

Programme the work and the project from the start and use the programme as a tool to manage the project, not just something that is stuck in a drawer and forgotten.

Set up standard project processes and follow them.

Keep in touch with your clients after the building work has been completed and ask occupants how they are finding living or working in the building. It is better to ask than let any problems rankle. Schedule time to speak to them periodically. Assuming the project went well you are likely to work with the client again or get a referral to another client.

Learn as much as you can from previous projects. Reuse what has worked well (designs, construction details, project processes, other consultants, contractors and so on) and where possible discard what has caused delay, proved to be a poor design decision or a business relationship that hasn't worked.

Stage 7

In Use

RIBA Plan of Work 2013 Stage 7

RIBA
Plan of
Work
2013

Stage 7

In use

Task Bar	Tasks
Core Objectives	Undertake **In Use** services in accordance with **Schedule of Services**.
Procurement Variable task bar	*There are no specific activities in the RIBA Plan of Work 2013.*
Programme Variable task bar	*There are no specific activities in the RIBA Plan of Work 2013.*
(Town) Planning Variable task bar	*There are no specific activities in the RIBA Plan of Work 2013.*
Suggested Key Support Tasks	Conclude activities listed in **Handover Strategy** including **Post-occupancy Evaluation**, review of **Project Performance**, **Project Outcomes** and **Research and Development** aspects. Updating of **Project Information**, as required, in response to ongoing client **Feedback** until the end of the building's life.
Sustainability Checkpoints	• *Has observation of the building operation in use and assistance with fine tuning and guidance for occupants been undertaken?* • *Has the energy/carbon performance been declared?*
Information Exchanges (at stage completion)	**'As-constructed' Information** updated in response to ongoing client **Feedback** and maintenance or operational developments.
UK Government Information Exchanges	As required.

Introduction

On average, practices spend 2% of their turnover on marketing. However, smaller practices fall below the benchmark: Micro: 1.3%; Small: 1.4%; Small to medium: 1.4%.

RIBA Business
Benchmarking Survey
2013/14

Stage 7 is a new stage for the Plan of Work 2013 and covers activities undertaken after completion of work carried out under the Building Contract.

(Note: the Defects Liability Period and Post-occupancy Evaluation activities are both part of Stage 6).

The stage involves:

— Activities associated with the maintenance of a building throughout its life, leading to potential alteration or refurbishment, bringing the Plan of Work 2013 cycle back to Stage 0.
— The opportunity to maintain a relationship with the client (or building user if these are different people) with a view to studying the building's performance for use on future projects and recognising the potential for further work or referrals from that client.

For most small projects it is unlikely that further fees will be attainable during Stage 7. However, all buildings need maintenance and this work could attract consultancy fees. Many buildings are altered and/or extended during their life and this will certainly attract consultancy fees. Stage 7 can be considered the period – during the life of the building – where a relationship with the client can be maintained. Remember that between one-third and three-fifths of commissions result from repeat business (depending on practice size). Add to this the potential for referrals by recommendation and it can represent a critical percentage of a practice's income.

23

Project activities

Information required

1.	'As-constructed' Information.
2.	BIM model (if one is available).
3.	Programme of maintenance.
4.	Terms of appointment for services to be undertaken.

Stage activities

1.	Periodically make contact with the building occupier and/or owner (if a different person or company) to ascertain any matters that need attention.
2.	Where possible agree fees for any work required.
3.	Where it is felt appropriate and of benefit, keep a record of the building's performance, both in environmental terms and with regard to durability of materials and the performance of construction detailing.

Making time for your clients

You will need to set time aside for these activities, but once they are standardised (perhaps within your QA system) they need not take up much time and will definitely add value. Set up reminders in your electronic diary and keep a note on your CRM spreadsheet; see advice on setting up a CRM programme in Stage 7: Client relationship management (CRM).

Information exchange

1.	'As-constructed' information updated in response to ongoing client Feedback and maintenance or operational developments.
2.	A record of client comments and Feedback, both objective and subjective.

On average, practices win 57% of the projects that they chase (53% for micro practices and 65% for small practices), including repeat business and projects won as a result of a direct approach with no competitive process.

RIBA Business
Benchmarking Survey
2013/14

Sustainability Checkpoint 7

Sustainability aims

To provide any services relevant to the operation or use of the building as agreed.

Key actions

1.	Observe the building operation In Use and assist with fine tuning and guidance for occupants.
2.	Check that the energy/carbon performance has been declared.
3.	Review controls and performance in each season and update manuals and records to reflect any changes.
4.	Feed lessons learned from the Post-occupancy Evaluation back to the client and project team.

Post-occupancy Evaluation (POE) on small projects

As noted above, many small projects will not have provision for these sorts of post-occupancy activities but with rising energy prices clients are increasingly interested in improving their building's environmental performance, and being able to offer these services will be helpful in these circumstances. It is a matter of record that environmental performance often falls short of the designed targets (refer to www.carbonbuzz.org). Consider proposing a fee for such activities that is a percentage of the energy saving generated through your input.

> **Architect:**
> Gillespie Yunnie
> Architects

Date completed:
March 2013

Construction cost:
£250,000

The Royal William Yard, housing the largest collection of Grade I listed military buildings in Europe, was designed as a secure site with only a single point of entry. A structure linking the far end of the Yard with the open green space of the peninsular above has always been a key part of the regeneration master-plan. This would enable residents to access the park and historic battlements at the top of the high retaining wall, and allow walkers to continue along the South West Coast Path route via a dramatic piece of architecture. The brief was to find an effective solution with the most impact using the limited funds available.

A simplified staircase was designed to reduce the archaeological impact and structural requirements. Constructed entirely from steel, the stair is completely recyclable at the end of its life and is lit with ribbon LEDs, making the entire electrical load only 150 watts for a major piece of public realm architecture.

Awards:
Winner of the AJ Small
Projects Sustainability
Award 2014
Winner - RIBA South
West Award.
Winner - RIBA South
West Small Project of
the Year Award.
Commendation - Civic
Trust.

A steel 'portal' cuts through the huge retaining wall and the cantilevered upper flight leads down to a concealed glass viewing-platform, revealing panoramic views over the Tamar Estuary across to Cornwall. At night the view changes, using concealed LED ribbon lights to wash the entire inner surfaces with an ever-changing river of colour in the otherwise dark, hard context of the old military site, reminiscent of seaside promenades across the country.

The project had to be procured in a matter of months due to its grant-funded nature. Close team working and a collaborative approach to design development between the architects, engineers and fabricators allowed this to happen in a series of short workshops, where every detail was examined for cost-effectiveness and appearance and resolved live on-screen.

Project issues

Keeping in touch

Dear [client's name/s],
PROJECT NAME

It has been 6 months/12 months* since we last spoke/corresponded* so this is just a quick note to check if you have any questions we might be able to answer on the operation or maintenance of the building, or if you have any comments – objective or subjective – on how you are finding living in/working in/using* it.

We use all the feedback we get from our clients on previous projects to guide our work on future projects, with the aim of continuously improving our work and delivering value to our clients, so any thoughts you can share will be very much appreciated.

And of course if you have any other projects under consideration, please do bear us in mind!

I'm pleased to say we have recently [add note on recent project completions, planning wins, awards, new members of staff, etc].

I look forward to hearing from you.

Kind regards,
[Your name]

* Delete as applicable

Using BIM models for FM

Practices that can provide BIM capability might consider marketing this for the purposes of facilities management (FM). This niche activity need not be on projects the practice has delivered, and the sort of clients it would be appropriate for are not likely to be those the practice works for. However, for those seeking to increase the size of project they can work on, such work will give exposure to larger clients and provide an 'in' to get on to their suppliers lists.

So who are these clients?

The key people to approach will be contractors. Look up the local offices of the larger ones that are likely to be undertaking Private Finance Initiative (PFI)-type projects. Other potential clients are housing associations and other residential landlords for new-build properties or end-user owner/occupiers.

What does the work involve?

You will need to have the capability to import the 'As Constructed' drawings from the project, maintain a secure copy of them, either on your office server (suitably backed up) or in the cloud. The as-built model will need to be adapted and refined and integrated with the FM software in order to manage the building – currently this is driven through scheduled inputs that are taken from the model, but around 75% of the information is not actually required. An FM model is therefore a 'skinny' as-built model, and a good FM model will need to be trimmed of all unnecessary information – a Stage 6/7 task.

You will need to agree a programme of workflow or alternatively an hourly rate for work to be undertaken to update the model. You will also potentially be responsible for alerting the facilities manager when assets need to be maintained or replaced.

It should be noted that most FM issues deal with M&E services, and any changes would need to be fed back into the model. It may be preferable to have a specialist do this. If an FM team is producing information to be updated within the model, then it might need a model manager – someone who can ensure all the information is updated correctly – in which case the lead designer is best placed to offer this service on an hourly basis.

Post-occupancy Feedback can be incorporated into the model – patterns of use and seasonal variations, elements and components that work well can be supplied as a packaged element for the next job. For further advice go to www.bimtaskgroup.org/bim4fm-group.

> Architect:
Jarmund Vigsnæs
Arkitekter and Mole
Architects

Date completed:
January 2010

This project was for Living Architecture, a trust set up to build holiday houses with the specific intention of making extraordinary architecture that can then be experienced by the public. Norwegian firm Jarmund Vigsnæs Arkitekter was selected in 2008 through a short competition process, and Mole Architects are the UK firm partnering with the international architects employed by Living Architecture. Both architects were separately employed by the client through all stages of the contract, with the architects working in partnership to deliver the project. Fee structures reflected the changing roles of the two architects, with Jarmund Vigsnæs starting with a higher proportion of the fee during design stages, reducing as Mole ran the job on site; during Stage 4 the fee split was equal.

Situated on the Suffolk coast in an area of outstanding natural beauty, the 220m² holiday house replaced a smaller existing building on the site. Nearby houses are predominantly single storey, with little consistency of style.

Planning issues that had to be overcome were primarily the need to design for flood resilience, and the scale of the building within its context. The architects' desire to make a house that expressed the contrasting quality of the open ground floor and attic bedrooms above was in part a response to the jumbled roofscape of nearby houses. Consultation and extensive negotiations with the conservation and planning officers proved vital and, alongside a robust design and access statement, ensured planning success.

The structure of the house is a hybrid. The lower floor is a tanked in situ concrete base, with a structural concrete core and a concrete first floor partially cantilevered from the core. The upper floor is manufactured from cross-laminated timber. The timber frame was manufactured by a specialist contractor who completed a 3D model which was shared with the design team prior to fabrication.

Practice issues

Client relationship management (CRM)

Keeping in touch with your old clients and developing new ones is critical to business development and maintaining a pipeline of projects. This is generally termed 'client relationship management' (CRM) and is best managed with a simple spreadsheet so that you can reorder the information, for example by company name, or contact name or by activity, sector or 'next contact due'. This may help with sending out targeted marketing information.

Under 'Activity' note whether a client, consultant (eg engineer, planning consultant, interior designer, etc) or other. Always use the same terminology so that you can sort the information into categories.

Under 'Building sectors' note the principal sectors they are involved in (eg residential, offices, retail, etc).

The 'Notes on last meeting/conversation' should contain enough detail for you to recall the contact's key business interests (eg building sectors), the key issues discussed and any actions arising, eg 'send details of previous projects'; 'put in touch with another contact'; 'undertake speculative design'; 'given go-ahead for project'; etc.

Make a note of when the next contact is due and put a reminder in your electronic diary (eg MS Outlook or Google Calendar).

This spreadsheet is a vital tool in your business development activities and must be kept up to date and monitored regularly. And make sure it is properly backed up by your IT system!

The spreadsheet should have the following headings:

Company

Contact name

Job title

Activity

Building sectors

Address

Email

Telephone

Notes on last meeting/conversation

Next contact due

Awards

It is worth considering whether a project may have the potential to be entered for an award from the outset of design activity. Keep this in mind as you prepare drawings. The following is a list of the principle awards for small projects:

RIBA Awards

Annual deadline: February
Web link: www.architecture.com/RIBA/Awards/Awards.aspx
Submission requirements: RIBA Chartered Members and International Fellows only.

The RIBA Awards programme champions and celebrates the best of British architecture, covering all sizes of project. Most relevant to small practices are the Small Projects Awards (for projects under £500,000) and the Stephen Lawrence Prize (for projects under £1m). The Stephen Lawrence prize is intended to encourage fresh talent.

CIAT Award for Excellence in Architectural Technology and CIAT Alan King Award (for projects under £750,000)

Annual deadline: July
Web link: www.ciat.org.uk/en/awards
Submission requirements: Open to all individuals and/or practices and projects of all sizes completed in the last five years. Submissions on no more than two A2 presentation boards and two A1 detailed design drawings, plus a summary report, on two sides of A4 (approximately 1000 words) to show how the criteria have been addressed.

AJ Small Projects Award

Annual deadline: December
Web link: www.architectsjournal.co.uk
Submission requirements: Entries must be completed during a set period (usually in the previous two calendar years, be under £250,000 contract value and must not have had significant coverage in the architectural press. Entry fee £60+VAT, plus 150 word description, at least eight photographs, five drawings and one working detail.

The AJ Small Projects Award celebrates design quality and ingenuity, rewarding architects who apply big ideas to small-scale commissions.

AJ Retrofit Awards

Annual deadline: May
Web link: www.retrofitawards.com
Submission requirements: For retrofitted and refurbished buildings in the UK; the focus is on extending the life of a building rather than demolition. Entry form asks for 500 words on the project and at least eight images and plans.

Entry fee: £299 + VAT

AR House Awards

Annual deadline: April
Web link: www.arawards.architectural-review.com
Submission requirements: Any single dwelling house built in the last five years; can be located internationally and there are no budgetary restrictions. Judging is anonymous and is based on images/plans etc to be presented on two A2-sized boards, along with 250 word text.

Entry fee: £375 (exc. VAT)

AR Emerging Architecture Awards

Annual deadline: September
Web link: www.emergingarchitecture.architectural-review.com
Submission requirements: Anything led by a qualified architect aged 45 or below. Buildings, interiors, landscaping, refurbishment, urban projects, temporary installations, furniture and product designs are all eligible. Judging is anonymous and based on images/plans etc on two A2-sized boards. Prize fund of £10,000 and work published in a special edition of the *Architectural Review*.

Price to enter: £199 + VAT

AR Future Projects Awards

Annual deadline: December
Web link: www.mipimarfutureprojects.com
Submission requirements: This is for unbuilt projects – can be on the drawing board or under construction. Judging is anonymous and based on images/plans etc on two A2-sized boards delete.

Building Awards – Small Project of the Year

Annual deadline: December
Web link: www.building-awards.co.uk
Submission requirements: Details on the project, including: testimonials, aesthetics, innovations, images and financial information, as well as company information.

Aims of the award: The Small Project of the Year Award is designed to celebrate outstanding examples of construction projects with a value of up to £5m.

BD Awards – Small Project Architect of the Year

Annual deadline: September
Web link: www.awards.bdonline.co.uk/small-non-housing-project-architect-of-the-year/
Submission requirements: This award recognises architects who are undertaking non-housing projects of a relatively small scale, whether new build or refurbishment. All projects must be under £1m in value. Entries should include one built project from the last three years, and a minimum of one other project either built or unbuilt. No more than four projects in total should be submitted. The judges will be looking for evidence of all-round design excellence and fitness for purpose over a body of work.

Price to enter: £99 + VAT per entry

BD Awards – One-off House Architect of the Year

Annual deadline: September
Web link: www.awards.bdonline.co.uk/individual-house-architect-of-the-year/
Submission requirements: This category is intended for one-off family houses of any budget. Entries should include one built project from the last three years, and a minimum of one other project either built or unbuilt. No more than four projects, in total, should be submitted. The judges will be looking for evidence of all-round design excellence and fitness for purpose over a body of work.

Price to enter: £99 + VAT per entry

> ## Stage summary

It is not usual – traditionally - for the design team to continue involvement with a building after its completion (that is after the Defects Liability Period) but Stage 7 provides a framework for this to happen. For small projects it is likely to be just keeping in touch (and therefore with no fee associated), with a view to picking up the next job, and it is more likely that only larger projects will provide a role for maintenance where a fee can be agreed.

However, information gained from Feedback can and should be fed into Stage 0 activities for future projects which could include further construction work associated with the same building.

Stage 0

Strategic Definition

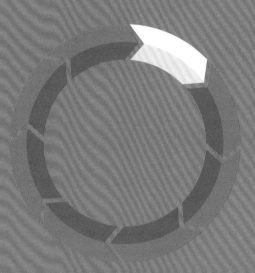

RIBA Plan of Work 2013 Stage 0

RIBA
Plan of
Work
2013

Stage 0

Strategic
Definition

Task Bar	Tasks
Core Objectives	Identify client's **Business Case** and **Strategic Brief** and other core project requirements.
Procurement Variable task bar	Initial considerations for assembling the project team.
Programme Variable task bar	Establish **Project Programme**.
(Town) Planning Variable task bar	Pre-application discussions *may be required to test the robustness of the* **Strategic Brief**.
Suggested Key Support Tasks	Review **Feedback** from previous projects.
Sustainability Checkpoints	• *Ensure that a strategic sustainability review of client needs and potential sites has been carried out, including reuse of existing facilities, building components or materials.*
Information Exchanges (at stage completion)	**Strategic Brief**.
UK Government Information Exchanges	Not required.

43

Introduction

Certain activities in Stage 0 are derived from the former Stage A of the Plan of Work 2007.

Stage 0 is a new stage for the Plan of Work 2013 and has been incorporated to ensure that the Business Case for the project is properly considered and a Strategic Brief developed.

It involves:

— Identifying the client's Business Case (if appropriate)
— Developing the Strategic Brief
— Considering the Project Programme
— Reviewing Feedback from previous projects
— Preparing and agreeing the scope of work and the appointment

For many small projects cost may not be the key determinant but it is always an important one. Value is always a key determinant of success and designers have a duty to understand what represents value to their clients and then to deliver it through well-considered and executed work. Value can only be determined through dialogue with the client to understand their needs, whether it is for a house extension or new dwelling, an office or retail fit-out or some form of building enclosure or built intervention for other purposes.

It can be argued that even a house extension has a Business Case: a homeowner seeking more space has the option of moving house as an alternative. (With current levels of SDLT this is unlikely to be a cheaper alternative but there may be other considerations such as the quality of space attainable.) There are many reasons why extension might be the better option but all options should be considered and this is the right time to do that.

Sometimes the client's needs may be best met not by building but by some other means. An office that needs additional space may be able to achieve it through different working practices like hot-desking. You may or may not get a fee-paying commission from such advice but you will certainly get a reputation for honesty and integrity and this may well be more valuable in the long term. You should always have the best interests of your client in mind and offer advice accordingly.

Making value judgements

When making a decision on behalf of your client put yourself in their shoes to determine the most appropriate way forward. This can be applied to many different circumstances from broad design decisions to the level of specification of fit-out or equipment to be installed.

Ask yourself: if you were paying for it, what would you do?

It is at this stage that the overall Project Programme should be considered and the likely composition of the design team agreed.

It was noted earlier in the book that knowledge gained from previous projects (during Stage 7) can be valuable to future ones, and Stage 0 is the time to assess what that might be.

Although not strictly part of a project stage, any projects not coming as the result of repeat work or a referral will derive from marketing and business development, and these critical activities are covered in this section of the book.

Project activities

Information required

1.	Initial client enquiry/requirements, to be formed into the Strategic Brief.
2.	Feedback from previous projects. *Refer to Stage 6.*
3.	Building sector (eg residential, office, retail, etc) knowledge – best practice data, benchmark projects, regulations, etc.
4.	Basic Site Information. *At this stage it may be sufficient to use facilities like Google Earth to get site dimensions (particularly if the work is speculative), but OS maps can be purchased cheaply and will give more accurate information. If site dimensions are estimated make this clear in any design submissions and develop the design such that it will not be invalidated following accurate measurement.*
5.	If in competition: practice profile, project data sheets, CVs and other marketing material.
6.	Office resource schedule. *Refer to Stage 0: Fee proposals and appointments and Stage 1: Project programming.*

Advice on giving advice

Remember that even if you provide pro bono work on a project without a written agreement, you may still be liable in tort for any errors in the advice you give.

Warn the client if you consider their aims unrealistic due to planning policy, site constraints, budgetary constraints, etc. Avoid the use of jargon and communicate in a straightforward manner. Try not to appear negative though, and look for solutions to overcome any problems you foresee.

Clients, particularly one-off, first-time ones such as homeowners, need advisors who are sympathetic, so develop a 'bedside manner' and make sure your advice is focused on their needs rather than your individual design ambition. Where these are the same thing you will have found a really great client – assuming they also pay the bills on time!

Stage activities

| 1. | Receive enquiry from potential client and review it carefully. |

| 2. | Make checks on client as appropriate to ensure they are bona fide and have the means to undertake the project. Establish the client's level of experience. |

Note: domestic clients are 'consumers' under the Unfair Terms in Consumer Contracts Regulations 1999, which imposes a greater requirement on the architect to make sure they fully understand the terms and conditions of the appointment. Refer to the advice in Stage 1: RIBA standard forms of appointment.

| 3. | Undertake resource assessment including that required in terms of the health and safety regulations and make decision to proceed accordingly. |

If you don't have the resources in-house consider collaborating with another practice rather than just declining the opportunity. Your considerations as to whether to accept the commission may include other matters such as whether it is likely to be a profit- or loss-making exercise and whether it fits with your overall business plan and profile for the practice. If you decide to decline, make a recommendation for another practice. In this way you will have helped the client and be owed a favour from the other practice. Naturally you will need to consider whether this course of action will give an unwanted advantage to the competition!

4.	If possible, arrange a meeting with the client to discuss their needs, particularly if you have not met them before, and arrange a preliminary inspection of the site.
	Make them aware of any CDM Regulations duties that they might have – dependent upon the type of project (see also action 9 below).
5.	Ascertain the individual (husband, wife, company director, etc) who will have authority to make decisions and issue instructions.
6.	Look up the relevant town planning policies. Refer to the planning page of the local authority's website and the Planning Portal (www.planningportal.gov.uk). If the building is in a conservation area or is listed, include the necessary activities/approvals in your proposal to the client.
7.	Check with your professional indemnity insurers if the project calls for services outside those covered by the policy. For example, if you are likely to engage other consultants directly, be called upon to give advice on self-build operations, or act as manager for a series of separate trades contracts. Cover could also be called into question because of the nature or scale of operations, or because of stipulations by the client as to the amount or duration of cover required.
	If you engage sub-consultants directly, check their competence and resources, particularly with regard to the CDM Regulations. Consider the use of RIBA Sub-consultant Agreement 2010 (2012 revision).
8.	Prepare and submit a proposal.
	Refer to Stage 0: Fee proposals and appointments and Stage 0: Letter contracts.
9.	Notify client of CDM responsibilities (where applicable) and make sure they understand their duties.
	Refer to Stage 0: CDM responsibilities (for clients).
10.	If in competition prepare pitch to client.
	Refer to Stage 0: Perfect pitch – selling your ideas.

11.	Negotiate terms and fee as necessary. On agreement of scope of work and fee, issue appointment documents and arrange for signing by both parties. Alternatively, set out the proposal letter with a space for the client to sign and date, acknowledging their agreement and then returning a copy to you.
12.	Assess whether the project will be undertaken using BIM and act accordingly. *Refer to Stage 3: BIM for small practices and Stage 3: IT management.*
13.	Determine whether any other architects have previously been involved and if so check their appointment has been properly terminated and notify them of your involvement.
14.	Visit the site and make a detailed site assessment..
15.	Prepare site appraisal for the purpose of determining the Strategic Brief.
16.	Undertake viability assessment as required. *Refer to Stage 1: Design development appraisals.*
17.	Prepare and agree Strategic Brief with the client. *Refer to Stage 1: Developing the brief and Stage 1: Project brief proforma.*

Dealing with project enquiries

Respond at once to approaches from potential clients and submit a practice statement if appropriate. If the project is of interest, ask for further particulars, including details of the selection process to be adopted.

Avoid spending unnecessary time on 'long shots' or unsuitable commissions. In particular, avoid being drawn into giving free advice after the initial consultation.

Assess carefully what the project will require in terms of practice resources before you quote a fee. Do you have the necessary skills and staff? Can they be made available for the particular programme? If it looks as if you will be overstretched, can you buy in skills or subcontract work? See Stage 0: Fee proposals and appointments for advice on project resource planning and a link to spreadsheets that can be used to help with this activity. Whether prepared manually or as a spreadsheet, this could provide essential information for a fee bid and be a useful tool for monitoring small jobs.

Refer to the RIBA and ARB codes of practice which can be found at www.architecture.com and www.arb.co.uk.

Information exchange

1.	Appointment documentation.
	Refer to Stage 1: RIBA standard forms of appointment, below.
2.	Strategic Brief.
	Refer to Stage 1: Developing the brief and Stage 1: Project brief pro forma.
3.	Initial site appraisal.

These need only have as much detail as is necessary to establish the range of options that could meet the client's aspirations. You should draw them in such a way that they can be easily understood by the client, but take care not to get into too much detail as this is likely to be wasteful of time and effort.

If you are in competition you will probably need to develop the option studies in greater detail to win the work, but the extent to which you undertake speculative work must be weighed against the anticipated overall benefit of winning the commission and the effect on other, fee-paying work you are already undertaking.

4.	Initial viability assessment/development appraisal.

Refer to Stage 0: Development appraisals.

This should also be a high-level study, using benchmark figures for land value, construction cost and other costs to arrive at the appraisal. Always be transparent in how you communicate this sort of work and caveat it as appropriate. Many projects will not need this sort of assessment but it is good practice to do it anyway.

5.	Relevant building sector information/benchmarking.

6.	Initial advice on consultant team.

Explain to the client what other input will be required and what consultants he/she will need to appoint and at what stage in the project.

Sustainability Checkpoint 0

There are no specific tasks listed in the RIBA Plan of Work 2013; however, if the Sustainability Aspirations are likely to impact on how the project is defined then they should be considered and included in the Strategic Brief.

Sustainability aims

Establish the client's Sustainability Aspirations so that these can be properly taken into account in developing the Strategic Brief and Business Case.

Key actions

1.	Ensure that a strategic sustainability review of client needs and potential sites has been carried out, including reuse of existing facilities, building components or materials.
2.	Review client requirements to distil their Sustainability Aspirations and the expected building lifespan against which capital costs and costs In Use should be balanced.
3.	Recommend inclusion of a Soft Landings approach to the project (www.bsria.co.uk/services/design/soft-landings).
4.	If the client is a business ask them to identify someone in a senior management position to be a sustainability advocate and/or appoint a sustainability champion within the project team. The client should also consider appointing a Soft Landings champion.
5.	Assess environmental opportunities and constraints of potential sites and building assets, including sufficient iterative modelling to support the conclusions of any Feasibility Studies.
6.	Initial consultation with stakeholders, identification of local planning sustainability requirements and appraisal of existing building, social, transportation, water, energy, ecological and renewable resources, including the need for pre-construction or seasonal monitoring or surveys, should be undertaken.
7.	Where appropriate, identify potential funding sources and their eligibility criteria.

Review relevant current and emerging EU, national and local sustainability policies and legislation and analyse their implications for building, environmental and performance targets.

8.	Identify and understand the final occupants' needs in order to help to establish user patterns, energy profiles and the performance standards required.
9.	Identify the planning authority's sustainability requirements.
10.	Where appropriate advise the client on the merits and protocols of using a BIM model to help deliver sustainability aims.

> **Architect:**
Project Orange

Date completed:
2012

Construction cost:
£360,000

Awards:
Shortlisted – AJ
Retrofit Awards 2014

The client for Eaton Terrace runs a monthly dining club from their home in central London. The brief was to design a small extension providing more living space for the family, and also to reconfigure the existing house to better accommodate guests.

The key move was to shift the kitchen to the first floor alongside the dining room and reintroduce partitions at ground floor level to create an office and snug.

To the rear of the house an infill extension with a huge roof light forms a new day room. Bedrooms, the master bathroom and a second study are located on the second floor, with the basement redesignated as the son's quarters. An original extension off the main staircase contains a guest WC and second bathroom at half landings.

Both the kitchen and built-in furnishings have been carefully designed using standard products but with detail nuances introduced to create a more quirky aesthetic. A new underfloor heating installation required the removal of the existing floorboards, which in turn were inventively re-used in the new furnishings and a bespoke door lining to the dining room was added.

Project issues

Development appraisals

Key to adding value to a design exercise is understanding how to 'optimise the asset'. If you are designing for a developer he/she will probably have considered the cost drivers before appointing the design team, but you should be able to talk with some understanding of their business model. In setting up the project and developing the brief you should consider the following matters:

Value (in £/ft² or £/m²) of similar properties in the local area. This will give you an upper level for the overall Project Budget (having deducted any developer's profit required).

Typical construction costs for the building type in that location.

Planning constraints on use class, size, parking/access, etc.

If appropriate, the relative cost of refurbishment versus new build for this project.

In terms of the design:

Carefully plan the layout to maximise 'net to gross', ie the amount of useable space against circulation space and space that cannot be let.

Design the building so that it can be adapted in the future. Note however that if the project is for a trader developer who plans to sell the building this should not be at the expense of optimising the current use.

Where appropriate, consider phased delivery. This will usually only apply to larger developments however.

Design buildings to minimise energy use and carbon content (ie embedded energy).

This way of thinking is just as relevant to a house extension as it is to a major town centre development. By making value judgements you will be spending the Project Budget where it has the most impact.

Of course there are other considerations which are more qualitative than quantitative and are key to producing good architecture, which itself brings value. Consideration of matters such as public realm, well-being and 'the masterly, correct and magnificent play of masses brought together in light' are also issues that affect value, albeit in a less well-defined way.

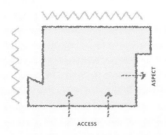

Site appraisal

Get a complete understanding of site constraints and opportunities before commencing design.

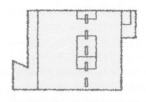

Adaptability

For speculative development provide the best fit for the largest number of potential end users. For commercial offices, maximise the potential for sub-division.

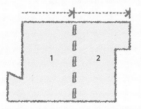

Phasing

Where appropriate design buildings that facilitate phased delivery.

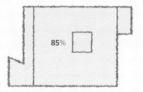

Net to gross

Buildings should be designed to maximise efficiency to avoid unnecessary capital expenditure.

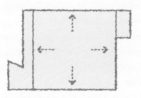

Optimising the site

Add value to the site by optimising the development potential and safeguarding the long-term investment value.

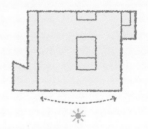

Energy efficiency

Design buildings to maximise energy performance to secure future value.

Fee proposals and appointments

Fees should be calculated following an assessment of the activities and deliverables required for each stage and the time and personnel necessary to undertake them. You can use the action checklists in this book as a starting point. In making this assessment you should take into account the cost rates for each individual *Refer to Stage 1: Project programming*. If assumptions are made, for example on the method of Procurement, these must be stated. It is recommended that you set out the proposal in as much detail as you are able and price individual stages. You should also note the timescale for each stage.

There are two distinct benefits of following this method:

— You will scope (and undertake) no more work than you are being paid for. Of course sometimes there will be a need to undertake speculative work in order to land a commission but you should always be aware of how much work is involved from the outset. This should be set out in writing and, ideally, a firm, written agreement should be obtained, confirming that should the project proceed you will be commissioned without competition. *Refer to Stage 0: Letter contracts.*
— You will have a means of demonstrating where additional work has been required, which will be valuable in any negotiations for an uplift in fees.

You should set out a cash flow forecast so that the client can budget his/her expenditure and to prevent argument as to when fees become due. This forecast can be adjusted if necessary during the course of the project should there be any delays. Where work stages are more than six weeks' duration it is advisable to set interim (typically monthly) payments.

When following this method of fee calculation it is advisable to check the total against previous projects and your understanding of what is typical in the profession. If the total is higher than you feel likely to achieve you will need to adjust the scope of work, or find efficiencies in the working method.

It is critical to set the fee at a level that is competitive but also allows you to undertake the project without risk. You should in any case work efficiently – refer to Stage 1: Lean thinking and creating value - and aim to do the routine activities as systematically as possible.

It is important to assess your costs, principally the time/staff-related ones, and ensure that you can make a sensible profit. Even if you are taking on a project for reasons other than financial ones (eg for publicity, competitions, etc) it is good practice to determine how much time (and therefore cost) you plan to spend, and monitor it.

Demonstrate value

When preparing your proposal take care to present it to the client in a manner that demonstrates the quantity of work required and the value you will be bringing to the project. The fee can then be explained and agreed with the client and can form the basis of a transparent and successful relationship.

The RIBA publishes a project fee calculator which has been prepared with small practices in mind and can be found at www.architecture.com. It consists of:

1. The fee calculator in MS Excel, comprising:
   a. A guide to using it and notes to assist with the documents produced.
   b. A programme generator using the RIBA Plan of Work stages.
   c. A resource calculator, to allow the practice to structure and understand its own costs.
2. A worked example.
3. Typical client questions and model answers – to provide a set of reliable answers to typical client questions about fees.
4. Practice pointers.

This method aims to ensure that architects charge appropriately for their services, mitigate the chances of making a loss, and help clients understand what is involved in the service and appreciate the professionalism that is demonstrated.

A web-based version is under development.

An alternative method of fee calculation can be found in the *RIBA Handbook of Practice Management 9th edition* (2013).

For very small projects (below around £100,000) a letter contract may be appropriate. The RIBA publishes *'A guide to letter contracts'*, and model letters for both domestic and business clients can be downloaded free of charge from www.ribabookshops.com/lettercontracts. Refer to the book for guidance notes.

There will be occasions when you feel it appropriate to undertake work on a speculative basis. In these circumstances it is important to record the terms on which the offer is made. The RIBA Code of Professional Conduct requires members to define the terms of engagement before services are provided, and not to make an offer of services unless invited to do so.

Letter contracts

An offer will provide the basis for a contract and should therefore:

— Be as carefully considered as any other proposal.
— Be addressed to the client.
— State what the offer comprises, the conditions that would apply on acceptance of the offer and to any subsequent appointment, and the liability for fees arising.
— Attempt to prevent exploitation of the architect by the client, particularly in respect of copyright.

While a contract requires 'offer and acceptance' to be complete, it may be reasonable to assume that a contract has come into force if, after receipt of an offer, the client actions imply acceptance. If no response is received, it will be another matter for the architect's commercial judgement on whether to proceed with the services.

 Note: if the response is 'Please get on with the services and we can negotiate', it could make the architect's position unclear, particularly over the terms of any future contract.

The letter should be written along these lines (see overleaf):

Dear [Name],
PROJECT NAME

We are obliged to comply with the RIBA Code of Conduct which prevents us from undertaking work without a written agreement as to the service offered and the fees to be charged. This letter provides a basis to comply with these requirements to cover the period until a more formal and explicit contract, as referred to below, can be executed.

We have agreed to undertake [note scope of speculative element of the work] on a speculative basis, but should work proceed beyond this stage fees will be payable as set out below.

[Set out proposal for appointment should the project proceed further.]

If these terms are acceptable, please sign the enclosed copy of this letter and return it to us. We shall then be in a position to start work. We are looking forward to working with you on this project.

Yours sincerely
[Your name]

I/We confirm that [practice name] is to proceed with the preliminary services as set out above.
[Signed]
[Client's name] [date]

RIBA standard forms of appointment

It is strongly recommended that you always use one of the standard forms of appointment published by the RIBA: Standard, Concise or Domestic Agreement exactly as recommended in the guidance notes set out in Guide to RIBA Agreements. If for whatever reason this is not possible, seek legal advice.

When setting out in writing the professional services to be carried out, make clear what is not included, leaving no room for misunderstanding. With a consumer client (such as on a domestic project) always arrange to meet and talk through the terms proposed in detail, and make sure the client fully understands them. If you do not, under the Unfair Terms in Consumer Contracts Regulations 1999 certain terms may not be considered to have been 'individually negotiated' and therefore become void. For domestic projects, use the *RIBA Domestic Project Agreement*.

See also Stage 0: Fee proposals and appointments and Stage 0: Letter contracts.

CDM 2015 – principal designer duties

1.	Discharge the duties of the CDM principal designer in compliance with the CDM Regulations 2015.
2.	Plan, manage, monitor and coordinate the pre-construction phase of the project, taking into account the General Principles of Prevention to ensure that so far as is reasonably practicable, the project is carried out without risks to health or safety.
3.	Provide assistance to the Client in the preparation of the Pre-Construction Information required by Regulation 5(2).
4.	Manage the design team to identify and then eliminate, or control, so far as is reasonably practicable, foreseeable risks to the health and safety of any person carrying out or liable to be affected by construction work; maintaining or cleaning a structure, or using a structure designed as a workplace.
5.	Facilitate cooperation of all persons working on the project.
6.	Monitor designers' compliance with their duties in Regulation 10.
7.	Provide Pre-Construction Information in a convenient form to every person designing the structure; and every Contractor who has been or may be appointed by the Client.
8.	Liaise with the principal contractor as appropriate for the duration of the project and in particular regarding any information which the principal contractor may need to prepare the Construction Phase Plan or which may affect the planning and management of the construction work.
9.	Prepare, and otherwise review and update the Health and Safety File, containing information relating to the project which is likely to be needed during any subsequent construction work to ensure the health and safety of any person, including the information provided in pursuance of Regulation 5(d) Client's duty in relation to the Health and Safety File; Regulation 10(3)(iii) Designers duty in relation to the Health and Safety File; Regulation 12(i) & (j) principal contractor's duty in relation to the Health and Safety File.
10.	At the end of the construction phase, issue the Health and Safety File to the Client. If the principal designer appointment ends before practical completion of the works, pass the H&S File to the principal contractor to complete.

CDM Regulations 2015 - clients

Domestic clients

CDM 2015 makes a distinction between domestic clients and commercial clients who commission construction work as part of their business. A domestic client is any individual who has construction work carried out on their home, or the home of a family member, that is not done as part of any business. While CDM 2015 places client duties on commercial clients in full, such duties for domestic clients normally pass to:

— the contractor, if it is a single contractor project, who must take on the legal duties of the client in addition to their own as contractor. In practice, this should involve little more than what they normally do in managing health and safety risks.
— the principal contractor, for projects with more than one contractor, who must take on the legal duties of the client in addition to their own as principal contractor. If the domestic client has not appointed a principal contractor, the client duties must be carried out by the contractor in control of the construction work.

If a domestic client has appointed an architect or other designer on a project involving more than one contractor, they can ask them to manage the project and take on the client duties instead of the principal contractor. This should be a separate appointment to that of architect/designer. The designer then takes on the responsibilities of principal designer and must have a written agreement with the client, confirming they have agreed (as principal designer) to take on the client duties as well as their own responsibilities.

Any designer in charge of coordinating and managing a project is assumed to be the principal designer. However, if they do not have a written agreement with the domestic client to confirm they are taking on the client duties, those duties automatically pass to the principal contractor.

Other clients

Other than domestic clients, all other clients have a duty to ensure that their construction project is set up so that it is carried out in a way that adequately controls the risks to the health and safety of those who may be affected. See checklist on page 69. You can also send your client a copy of the HSE/CITB document 'Industry Guidance for Clients' which can be downloaded free of charge (search the title to find a pdf copy). See also 'Industry Guidance for Principal Designers'.

Client CDM checklist

This checklist can be sent to (non-domestic) clients to inform them of their duties

CDM 2015 client duties	Tick
Are you clear about your responsibilities?	
Have you made your formal appointments?	
Have you checked that the principal designer or designer has the capability and necessary skills, knowledge, training and experience to fulfil their duties?	
Have you checked that the principal contractor or contractor has the capability and necessary skills, knowledge, training and experience to fulfil their duties?	
Have you checked that the project team is adequately resourced?	
Has a project or client brief been issued to the project team?	
Has the project team been provided with information about the existing site or structure (pre-construction information)?	
Has project-specific health and safety advice been sought?	
Are there suitable arrangements to manage health and safety throughout the project?	
Has a schedule of the key activities for the project been produced?	
Has sufficient time been allowed to complete the key activities?	
Where required, has an online F10 notification form been submitted to HSE to notify them of commencement of work?	
Have you checked that a construction phase plan has been adequately developed before work starts on site?	
Are you satisfied that suitable welfare facilities have been provided before work starts on site?	
Have you agreed the format and content of the health and safety file?	

Architect:
West Architecture

Date completed:
February 2010

Form of contract:
JCT Minor Works

Construction cost:
£140,000

Photography:
Peter Cook

Therefore are a product design consultancy based in Fitzrovia, London. West Architecture were appointed to reorganise their meeting, break-out and arrival spaces while upgrading staff facilities and improving the street presence of the company. Previously on arrival visitors entered a small lobby with no clear indication of where to go or wait. The ground floor held a single meeting room and waiting area isolated from the rest of the building through a series of doors and lobbies, whilst all office floors were served by a single small kitchen in the basement with no common space. All of this combined to reinforce the sense of separation between the various elements of the company.

Influenced by the client's role as product designers and as such the designers of objects, the architects sought to create a series of spaces that were clearly defined by highly detailed objects. The ground floor became a large single volume treated as four separate rooms which can be connected and disconnected both functionally and physically as required. As well as providing facilities for meetings and presentations the ground floor is now the social hub of the company. New glazed openings to the street with solid timber vents are framed in an aluminium sleeve which echoes some of the original features of the existing building.

The main space is articulated by three timber elements, two of which close off the meeting area while the third conceals a fire curtain and becomes a lobby in the event of a fire. They are all constructed from oak veneered 40mm 'Triply' and were manufactured outside the main contract by the client's own workshop team to West Architecture's design. The collaborative approach to these elements resulted in an end product which relied heavily on handcrafting, testing and finishing; something that would have been prohibitive in terms of costs under a standard designer-contractor relationship.

The sliding screens are mutually supported back to a fixed end panel negating the need for a bottom track. Stability is also increased by hanging them at their precise centre of gravity. Inside the main meeting room the screen is battened to improve acoustics.

Practice issues

SWOT analysis

In order to improve your 'offer' to clients it is important to know your strengths and weaknesses ('internal' matters) and what are the opportunities and threats to your business ('external' matters). This is collectively known as a SWOT analysis, and for a start-up practice adopting a collaborative approach to project work it might look like this:

Strengths

Good client contacts from previous work experience.

Good knowledge and relevant experience of residential, retail and office sectors.

Low overheads through working from home and dealing with projects through collaboration with other practices.

Broad reach and scale through collaboration.

Recognised ability to optimise a site's potential.

Weaknesses

No employees, so limited ability to react quickly to opportunities.

No office premises, so have to hold client meetings 'off site'.

Unrecognised brand.

Limited sector spread.

Limited IT skills, so heavy reliance on others for drawings, 3D modelling, etc.

Opportunities

Gaining publicity through writing magazine articles and RIBA publications.

Building a presence in residential market based on association with collaborators in the sector.

Ability to manage own time and get better work/life balance.

Threats

Competition from other small practices.

Not being able to find a collaborator for a particular project.

Missing the buzz of working in a large practice on large projects.

Keep to the main points but be honest. This is a document only you will see – it is not for external consumption. Review it at regular intervals and at least annually.

Setting up an efficient practice

Before you can start producing projects effectively you need the backbone of a well-set-up practice, and it is worth investing time in getting this right. Other than paying financial dividends over the course of time it will also give you a more professional public face and help to manage risk. Successful practice is as much down to the working environment and business structures you create around you as it is being a good designer. Key matters to address are:

— Having a well-considered set of QA procedures (whether you choose to be accredited or not).
— Maintaining a schedule of projects, income, cash flow and resource needs.
— Setting up and maintaining a core group of collaborators who are trusted and with whom you can work successfully.
— Generating and managing a supply chain for design services (eg other consultants), contractors and products suppliers that provide high-quality, good-value goods and services.
— Having a clear programme for marketing and business development that is time-bound and well-managed and based on the skills and capabilities of the practice and its collaborators.
— Having clear HR policies (for those employing staff) that enable you to attract and keep the best candidates.
— Developing appropriate BIM capabilities.
— Developing and maintaining a thorough knowledge of the sectors the practice focuses on.
— Regularly reviewing the practice's core aims and ambitions and making adjustments as necessary to reflect any changes in the economic and construction industry climate.
— Recognising what your strengths are and focusing on those areas.

Finding and keeping clients

Marketing is key to a successful business and involves listening to what your clients want, defining what you can offer to them to fulfil that need and selling that capability to them.

So first you should ask 'who are my potential clients?' Concentrate on those most likely to deliver paid work (measured in quality – eg paying on time – as well as quantity).

Determine what your 'DNA' is and make sure it is visible in everything you do in your marketing initiatives.

Elevator pitch

Prepare an 'elevator pitch' that summarises everything you want to say about you and your practice in an interesting way in no more than 30 seconds. Even if you don't find many opportunities to actually put it to use it is a valuable exercise to help get your intended direction clear in your own mind, and also to help communicate this to your colleagues, employees and collaborators, as well as your clients.

An elevator pitch

Hawkins\Brown is a multi-award winning architectural practice and currently AJ Practice of the Year.

Our expertise covers a range of building types across new developments and regeneration programmes.

People are at the centre of everything we do, from our studio ethos to focusing on the building's users, and we put our hearts and minds into realising every project's potential.

For nearly three decades, we've been making buildings with our clients from the inside out.

We believe that an approach, not a house style, produces better places.

We are open and design-led but our approach is always rigorous and thoroughly researched. You'll discover creativity, commitment and a desire to collaborate to reach the best solution.

The way we work, live, learn, travel and gather is changing, and the boundaries are blurring. Our experience across sectors will make sure you get the most out of your site.

If someone asks what you do, cite examples where you have won planning permission, optimised the value of a site, or delivered the project on time and within budget, for example.

The core aims of the practice that you might cite could include:

Having an opinion but no preconceptions.

Initiating ideas and solving problems.

Structured, creative thinking and clear communication.

A client focus – listening, not assuming or presuming.

Being reliable and having integrity.

Leadership and taking responsibility.

Being approachable and open and embracing collaboration.

Commercial understanding and managing risk.

Adopting lean processes and continuous improvement.

Sustainability and having respect.

Understanding value and optimising the asset.

Seeing the wood for the trees.

Client perception study

To understand what your clients think of you, consider undertaking a client perception study. This not only gives you valuable insight but tells your clients that you are focused on their needs and prepared to adapt to improve the service you offer. The sort of questions you ask might include:

What do you look for in your architects?

What do we do well?

What could we do better?

Where do you feel we have delivered value?

Where, if anywhere, do you feel we have failed to provide what you had expected to be delivered?

Create a list that looks into the sort of services you have provided or look to provide. Keep it short so that people are not put off completing it. It should take them no more than five minutes altogether – let them know this.

The RIBA Client Liaison Group initiated a client survey in 2016, 'Working with Architects', and the results have some invaluable information to help you understand what clients expect from their designers. The report, 'What Clients Think of Architects' can be found at www.architecture.com (go to 'Professional Support', then 'RIBA for Clients'.

Winning work (business development)

Whilst the two are closely related, business development is a separate series of activities to marketing. Whereas marketing is more broadly focused and deals with market research, brand management and getting your core messages out into the market place, business development is targeted at the important matter of landing the next job.

How much time do architects spend on winning work?

The average fee earners' time spent pitching for work is 13% for small practices, which equates to around five hours/week/person. This is a significant overhead so must be undertaken as efficiently as possible.

In practice it can be difficult to find time for these 'off-line' activities in between pressing project deadlines. However, they are critical to running a successful business, so set aside a particular part of the day (or week) to make the necessary preparations, send emails and make phone calls and do your utmost to stick to it.

Key contacts

The most successful businesses are often based on relatively few long-term key clients and it is worth investing time in these individuals and developing a depth of understanding about their business needs and plans. Bear in mind that clients could be contractors, other construction professionals or indeed other architects in a collaborative or sub-consultancy agreement. In that case, make sure there is a clear understanding, set out in writing, about the split of work and duties and the responsibilities of each party.

Networking

The construction industry is built upon relationships, and having a good personal network is essential for long-term success. The key to successful networking is not to look for short-term opportunities from a particular event (it doesn't work that way!), but to meet as many people as possible and look for ways you can help them – such as by giving advice, introducing them to someone useful to them and so on. This will ultimately form strong relationships that may, in the future, provide opportunities.

Using the CRM spreadsheet (see Stage 7) you should keep in touch with your key contacts, prioritising those most likely to give you work.

Conferences

Another way to meet people is by attending conferences and exhibitions within your target sectors/spheres of interest. However, enrolment fees for conferences can be high, added to which there is the time lost out of the office earning fees; so although they can be an excellent way of meeting relevant new people and gleaning the latest thinking on a particular subject, they must also return the value of investment, so choose which ones to attend carefully.

Speaking at conferences is always worthwhile and will reinforce your credentials in that sector. If you are interested in this sort of activity get in touch with conference organisers and let them know what you could contribute to future events.

R&D

As an alternative to a general practice brochure, consider identifying a potential project, for example to prepare proposals for developing derelict or under-used land, or finding new uses for redundant buildings and then to target specific clients on the strength of the proposed scheme. You must however consider how much time you can afford to spend on such an exercise, and stick to it. Make use of any specialisms you have and focus on these, eg sustainability, retrofit, restoration, specific building sectors and so on.

Competitions

Competitions can provide opportunities that would not otherwise be open to small practices, but be clear in your mind why you are doing them and what outcome you are hoping for. Plan what resources will be required to do the job properly, and only go for projects you have a reasonable chance of winning or will, at least, provide good marketing material from the design output.

Perfect pitch – selling your ideas

As an architect you have got to be able to design, to speak convincingly and to take instructions.

Tim Bailey
xsite architecture

1. Allow time for preparation

Don't short-cut preparation time so that you have to 'ad lib' on the day. Preparation is not just knowing what you want to say but also being prepared to answer questions, so make sure you know as much about the background to the project and the building type as the client does.

2. Preconceptions count

By the time you stand up to speak you have already missed your greatest opportunities to influence the outcome. These include correspondence before the meeting, the way you walk into the room and introduce yourself and what you say while you set up for the presentation. Take care to remember people's names and use them when you say goodbye at the end. Don't repeat them too often during the pitch however as this can appear patronising. Research shows that perceptions are enormously influenced by tone of voice and appearance, as well as visual imagery. In reality only a small proportion of the words spoken are actually remembered in detail.

3. Show you care

The project must be as important to you as it is to your client and you must demonstrate to them that you have the right attitude and care enough to deliver them value and creativity. Ask questions and centre the pitch on their needs, keeping it relevant. Don't focus too much on you – other than the project itself, show them you know about their business, competitors, history and goals and what is important to them.

4. Keep to the allotted time

Don't just keep talking until the interviewer tells you your time has run out. Take care to listen closely to any questions and answer them carefully, but once you've finished the pitch, don't continue trying to sell. Always follow up with a brief email or letter saying how much you enjoyed meeting them and look forward to the opportunity of working with them. You can also reiterate the key messages of the pitch, but don't overdo it.

5. Reinforce your brand

You should always take the opportunity to reinforce your core messages so as to give consistency and help potential customers understand where you sit in the industry and what your key offer is.

Web design advice

A well-designed website is the single most important weapon in your marketing arsenal. It is the first place a potential client will look for background on your experience and capabilities. Its design will need to reflect your brand – are you a high-end, creative design studio, a practice specialising in the production and construction stages or one that preaches the importance of the same practice following the project from concept to completion? There is no right or wrong way.

A simple website can be built using off-the-shelf packages such as Adobe Dreamweaver (www.adobe.com/products/dreamweaver) or Serif (www.serif.com).

A space to host the website will also be needed, and a domain name registered (companies such as www.fasthosts.co.uk offer packages incorporating both of the above as well as the facility to check whether a chosen domain name is available).

Alternatively, free online tools such as Google Sites (www.google.com/sites/help/intl/en/overview.html) or blog platforms such as Wordpress (www.wordpress.org) provide quick and relatively easy methods of creating a web presence.

Without proper web design experience or knowledge of setting up a web space and domain, a website can lack a professional feel, and look amateurish in comparison to those of your competitors. If budget allows, it is best to use a professional website designer to build a bespoke site to a design brief.

Using specific keywords and additional tools such as Google Analytics (www.google.com/analytics) can also increase visits to a site. Once a website is up and running, depending upon its functionality, this can be used as a tool for embedding email shots and other promotional tools.

Creating impact on your website

Your website is probably the most important means of communicating with your clients and prospective clients, collaborators and so on. Remember the following points when designing it.

Look at the websites of architects you admire or who are providing a similar service to yourself to get ideas.

The homepage should be memorable and say something about the practice. Some websites have little more than an intriguing image and a link to the site; others choose to present critical information such as contact details and a summary note on what the practice does. Decide what sort of practice you aspire to be and select a suitable approach, but whatever you do it should aim to differentiate you from the competition. The homepage must say at a glance what your business is, what sort of work it aims to produce and the way it goes about producing it (eg are you design-focused or process-focused, front-end or 'executive' architects – or all of these, and what geographic areas do you cover?).

Make sure visitors to the website can navigate and find what they want easily and quickly. Draw a map of all the pages you want and how they are to be connected. Make sure visitors can get back to the homepage from any other page. Make the page structure simple to understand, and if your contact details are not on the homepage make them easy to locate. Try to follow the three-click rule: that a user of a website should be able to find any information with no more than three mouse clicks.

Only show images (possibly including drawings) of your projects that reinforce your brand and only use the best ones. Set them out by sector and/or date. Don't write long descriptions; people don't generally spend more than a minute or two browsing a website, so rely on the images to tell the story.

Adding share buttons is a simple way of optimising your design for social networks. Blogging is another way of keeping in touch with your network, but make sure you update your blog pages regularly.

> ## Stage summary

This stage is all about setting off on the right foot. To do that you need to understand your client (where possible, spend time to get to know them), understand everything about the site and the building type, have standard office and project systems in place and establish an agreed, written appointment. If you do this you have every chance of developing a well-conceived building, making a profit and developing a sound relationship with your client. Cut corners and you will always be open to errors. As the adage goes, 'a stitch in time saves nine'.

The Strategic Project Brief and initial Feasibility Studies developed in Stage 0 will be developed into the Initial Project Brief and (ideally) a single, preferred design option during Stage 1.

Stage 1

Preparation & Brief

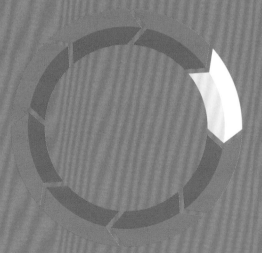

RIBA Plan of Work 2013 Stage 1

RIBA
Plan of
Work
2013

Stage 1

Preparation
and Brief

Task Bar	Tasks
Core Objectives	Develop **Project Objectives**, including **Quality Objectives** and **Project Outcomes**, **Sustainability Aspirations**, **Project Budget**, other parameters or constraints and develop **Initial Project Brief**. Undertake **Feasibility Studies** and review of **Site Information**.
Procurement Variable task bar	Prepare **Project Roles Table** and **Contractual Tree** and continue assembling the project team.
Programme Variable task bar	Review **Project Programme**.
(Town) Planning Variable task bar	*Pre-application discussions may be required during this stage to discuss and determine the suitability of **Feasibility Studies**.*
Suggested Key Support Tasks	Prepare **Handover Strategy** and **Risk Assessments**. Agree **Schedule of Services**, **Design Responsibility Matrix** and **Information Exchanges** and prepare **Project Execution Plan** including **Technology** and **Communication Strategies** and consideration of **Common Standards** to be used. *The support tasks during this stage are focused on ensuring that the project team is properly assembled and that consideration is given to the handover of the project and the post-occupancy services that are required.*
Sustainability Checkpoints	• *Confirm that formal sustainability targets are stated in the **Initial Project Brief**.* • *Confirm that environmental requirements, building lifespan and future climate parameters are stated in the **Initial Project Brief**.* • *Have early stage consultations, surveys or monitoring been undertaken as necessary to meet sustainability criteria or assessment procedures?* • *Check that the principles of the **Handover Strategy** and post-completion services are included in each party's **Schedule of Services**.* • *Confirm that the Site Waste Management Plan has been implemented.*
Information Exchanges (at stage completion)	**Initial Project Brief.**
UK Government Information Exchanges	Required.

Introduction

Stage 1 merges the residual tasks from the former Stage A of the Plan of Work 2007 with the Stage B tasks that relate to carrying out preparation activities and briefing in tandem.

Stage 1 can be considered as the final part of setting up the project for success.

It involves:

— Developing the Strategic Brief into the Initial Project Brief.
— Considering the composition of the Project Team and appointing any members needed for the initial stages of the project.
— Preparing the Project Programme and identifying the project deliverables.
— Developing design options that reflect the range of solutions that could meet the Strategic Brief and help to inform the Initial Project Brief.

For all projects, but particularly small ones, it is essential that a clear scope of work is agreed for optimum efficiency and to ensure that precious time is not wasted on activities that don't add value. See Stage 1: Lean thinking and creating value.

Time spent getting the brief right is time well spent that will pay dividends further down the line.

Project activities

Information required

1.	Site data, including: — Ordnance Survey map. — Site and/or building survey drawings. — Notes, sketches and photographs made during initial visits.
2.	Initial site appraisal.
3.	Strategic Project Brief. This should include the client's requirements, budget, project timetable and timetable for services.
4.	Relevant building sector information, regulations, etc.
5.	Relevant planning policy documents.
6.	Building Information Modelling (BIM) strategy.
7.	If available, health and safety file for the existing building with information on site hazards or references to work carried out previously.

Stage activities

1.	Open project files and allocate a job number to the project in accordance with office practice.
2.	Agree the Schedule of Services, Design Responsibility Matrix and Information Exchanges.

Check the scope of professional services agreed with other consultants as they are appointed to ensure there are no gaps in the service provided to the client.

Use the Design Responsibility Matrix in the RIBA Plan of Work 2013 Toolkit available free at www.ribaplanofwork.com.

3.	Prepare a Project Programme.

Refer to Stage 1: Project programming.

4.	Obtain from the client the project requirements, budget and timetable and any other project data being supplied by the client. Check these carefully, question incompatibilities and agree priorities.

Alert the client straight away to key issues that may be missing from these requirements and will need to be addressed in the Initial Project Brief, such as strategy for accessibility, security policy and environmental policy.

5.	Explain to the client the options for Procurement and note any matters which could affect the particular choice.

Refer to 'Which Contract?' 5th Edition (2012) for advice on this.

6.	Develop the town planning strategy.

Check the planning situation with the local planning authority. For example:

— Whether there is any existing relevant permission, approval or consent which is still current.
— Whether the proposed work requires planning permission, and if so which applications would be relevant.
— Whether there are special circumstances that need to be taken into account (eg listed building, conservation area, enterprise zone, development corporation).
— Whether an environmental impact assessment will be expected.
— Whether there is a known existence of hazardous substances or conditions due to earlier uses, likelihood of archaeological remains, etc.

— Whether there are plans for compulsory purchase or any land take proposals (eg for road improvements) which could affect use of the site.

| 7. | Undertake or procure a measured survey as appropriate. If the client is procuring the survey, assist in ascertaining the scope of it to make sure it encompasses everything that will be needed. |

Note: the survey should only be procured and undertaken once a built project has been determined to be necessary, or likely to be necessary.

Refer to Stage 1: Surveys.

It is also good practice to ascertain ground conditions early as this can substantially alter the design and would be problematic after planning permission had been granted. An initial idea of ground conditions can sometimes be found by consulting the local Building Control department.

| 8. | Obtain information on the existing mains services supplies. |

| 9. | Obtain information on the existing traffic/highways/access conditions. |

| 10. | Check whether there are restrictions on site development potential due to mains or cables either below ground or overhead, and whether or not the site is subject to easements or wayleaves. |

Check the position and capacity of mains drainage and services supplies from statutory undertakers. Alert the client at an early stage if it appears that there may be issues concerning the development that may require approval/agreement of adjoining owners, eg whether rights of light, boundaries, rights of way, such as for fire escapes or access, will be affected.

Note: these will normally be dealt with by the client's solicitors, but they may take a considerable time to negotiate.

11.	Check whether notices under the Party Wall etc Act 1996 may be needed.
	Refer to Stage 4: Party wall procedures.
12.	Check whether third parties, eg landlord, estate surveyor, lessees, adjoining owners, etc, will need to be consulted. Initiate preliminary consultations (if this is part of your agreed duties) when authorised by the client.
13.	Review the Site Information and prepare Feasibility Studies.
14.	Develop the client's requirements into an Initial Project Brief, or assist the client in developing an Initial Project Brief.
	Preparation of the Initial Project Brief is an important task and the time required to prepare it will depend on the complexity of the project. See notes on brief preparation below in this stage.
15.	Develop the Project Objectives, including Quality Objectives and Project Outcomes, risk profile, Sustainability Aspirations, Project Budget and other parameters or constraints. Refer to Guide to Using the RIBA Plan of Work (2013).
16.	Advise the client on the need to appoint a cost consultant and other consultants or specialists. Confirm who will make the appointments, the basis of agreements and the scope of such services. List the other consultants in the appointment agreement and any project quality plan.
	Be clear about the professional services needed. If other consultants and specialists are needed, be prepared to explain their roles and responsibilities. The guidance to the RIBA Plan of Work 2013 may be a useful tool at this stage for mapping out the tasks that must be performed and identifying who will perform them, although it should be noted that it may not list all appointments that are needed.
	Try to secure the client's consent that all professional appointments are on mutually interlocking agreements with similar, if not identical, contractual conditions. RIBA Agreements are available in architect and consultant versions with identical conditions, but Schedules of Services may be required for some disciplines.

17.	Advise the client on statutory and other legal obligations, including:

— The need for various approvals under national legislation concerned with planning and building, and the additional requirements of any local legislation or legislation for the particular building type which might apply.

— The fees payable to the relevant authority at the time of these applications.

— The obligations of a client under the CDM Regulations, and other health and safety legislation, as appropriate including the need to appoint a principal designer, where the law requires this (if not already done).

— See pages 12 and 67-69 for advice on the CDM Regulations.

— The duties of the client as building owner under the Party Wall etc Act 1996, including the possible need to appoint a party wall surveyor and the rights of adjoining owners to appoint their own surveyors.

— Possible duties of the client under Part IIA of the Environmental Protection Act 1990, if the site may contain contaminated land.

18.	Check whether any information provided by the client is confidential, and enquire whether the client wishes to ensure confidentiality for the project. If not, and publicity is sought, is this likely to involve wider consultation, eg presentations to a user client or local amenity bodies?

19.	Establish procedures for the client to 'sign off' briefs, designs, etc at relevant stages. Be strict about keeping to deadlines for reports and other submissions to the client. Set firm dates for approvals, instructions to proceed and the supply of information.

20.	Assemble the project team and define the members' roles and responsibilities and the Information Exchanges.

The importance of properly establishing the project team cannot be overstated given the increasing use of technology, which enables remote communication and project development using BIM. For Stage 2 to commence in earnest, it is essential that the team is properly assembled. The tools necessary to achieve this, and to produce the various documents required to accompany each team member's appointment, are considered in greater detail in Guide to using the RIBA Plan of Work 2013.

The RIBA Plan of Work 2013 advocates the definition and establishment of the project team during Stage 1. This ensures that the roles and responsibilities of each organisation are clear before commencement of Stage 2: Concept Design. The publication Guide to Assembling a Collaborative Project Team *(2013) provides advice on this process.*

| 21. | Confirm the design team composition and identify a project lead and lead designer. |

| 22. | Where appropriate, and in accordance with the project's Technology Strategy, appoint an information manager, whose role should include the following:
— Explaining to the client the benefits and implications of implementing BIM.
— Advising on the extent to which BIM should be used on the project.
— Determining the roles and responsibilities of each member of the project team with regard to the BIM process and the model.
— Leading other consultants in preparing the BIM project plan.
— Defining and communicating the BIM inputs and outputs.
— In conjunction with the other consultants, reviewing and signing off the model at agreed stages.
— Issuing data from the model at the appropriate times.
— Liaising with the contractor, subcontractors and suppliers to integrate their design data into the model.
— Arranging for the model to be passed on to the client's facilities manager at Practical Completion (unless the architect is to maintain a role in this regard). |

For further advice on working with BIM, refer to the RIBA publications BIM Demystified, 2nd Edition *(2012) and* Information Exchanges: RIBA Plan of Work 2013 Guide *(2014).*

| 23. | If appointed as information manager:
— Prepare BIM protocols and agree them with the other members of the design team.
— Define the responsibilities of the other members of the design team in this regard.
— Define long-term responsibilities, including ownership of the model.
— Define BIM inputs and outputs and scope of Post-occupancy Evaluation (Soft Landings). |

Refer to Stage 3: BIM for small practices.

24.	Establish or review project quality management procedures together with relevant procedures for all design team members. Consider preparing a Project Execution Plan and agree its format with the client and design team. *Note: whilst normally associated with larger projects, this need not be a complex or lengthy document and is a useful reference to ensure all members of the Project Team understand the scope and programme of the project and their responsibilities and the communication procedures to be followed.* *Refer to Stage 2: Project plan pro forma.*
25.	Agree working methods and procedures with the design team members, including: — Means for integrating and coordinating work and inputs. — Compatibility in systems, software, etc. *Refer to Stage 3: BIM for small practices.*
26.	Establish a programme and pattern for design team meetings. Where applicable the principal designer should be included to provide advice and assistance to both client and design team.
27.	Hold preliminary discussions with the planning officer to discuss key issues arising from the above checks. Establish the approach of the planning officer towards the principle of development as proposed and enquire whether serious difficulties might be expected. *It is advisable to seek the opinion of the local authority planning officer at an early stage in design development. Many authorities charge for this pre-application service, but it will give valuable feedback before the greater cost of developing the design and making a full application, and will help to manage risk in the planning process.*

The officer will give advice on planning policy and the likely outcome of an application. They may make recommendations to improve the chances of success if this is thought necessary. The process usually requires a set of drawings and other supporting information to be sent, with the fee (if one is required), following which a meeting will be arranged. A formal response will usually be issued shortly after the meeting, although it should be noted that the planning committee will not always follow the officer's recommendation.

The more information that is submitted, the greater the detail of advice you will receive in response; however, it is important not to present the proposals as a finished design but rather as design options, exploring a range of solutions that could meet the client's brief. This will tend to elicit the most beneficial response and demonstrate a willingness to involve the authority as a stakeholder. Matters such as planning policy, the local built environment, access and egress, bulk and massing of the proposal, building materials and sustainability targets should all be explained.

www.planningportal.gov.uk is a useful source of advice for all matters related to planning and making planning applications.

Refer also to Town Planning: RIBA Plan of Work 2013 Guide (2014).

28.	Submit applications (if instructed by the client) with relevant documents, including a cheque, credit card or BACS payment by the client for the appropriate fee.
29.	Monitor office expenditure against fee income: — Set up office procedures for recording time spent on the project, by whom and the rates chargeable, and for noting expenses and disbursements incurred. — Set up procedures for regularly checking expenditure against the office job cost allocation.
30.	Arrange for regular reports to be provided to the client on fees and expenses incurred, and for accounts to be submitted at agreed intervals.
31.	Inspect information provided by the client, including the health and safety file, if applicable. It is important to identify at the earliest possible stage whether there are

special conditions which will affect the viability of the project, eg contaminated land, asbestos in existing buildings.

| 32. | Consult with stakeholders as authorised. |

Note: consultations with users and some third parties do not form part of the services under the RIBA Standard Agreement unless identified under Part 3 'Other Services'. Third parties mentioned by the agreement and therefore not requiring identification under 'Other Services' include landlords and freeholders and others in that class (item 12) and those involved in negotiations in connection with statutory approvals (item 11).

| 33. | Together with other consultants, review the client's budget figures and identify the sums included for construction work. |

Review the client's requirements, programme and budget to assess compatibility. If they are not in balance, report this to the client and seek clarification on priorities.

| 34. | Provide information for the construction cost estimate . The report on cost implications should be structured under appropriate headings. It will normally be prepared by the cost consultant, if appointed. On jobs where there is no cost consultant, construction cost estimates may need to be prepared by the architect – the appointment must make this clear. |

| 35. | Prepare Stage 1 report which should contain the information from Stage 0 plus: |

— Initial Project Brief (as an update to Strategic Project Brief).
— Town planning appraisal.
— Feasibility Studies with recommendation for preferred option, plus justification.
— Feasibility report, to include development appraisal information as required.
— Preliminary Cost Information/appraisal.
— Target Project Programme.
— Environmental sustainability targets.
— Note on Procurement options and preferred option.

Information exchange

1.	Stage 1 report/Feasibility Study.

The Feasibility Study will establish the basis upon which the project should proceed. It may be that the job is not feasible at all, or that the client's requirements, programme and cost limits cannot be reconciled. The report should analyse and appraise needs, give an environmental assessment and offer possible options, together with recommendations for the way forward. It will probably include conceptual drawings and diagrams. Make sure the report is comprehensive, soundly researched and objective.

2.	The Initial Project Brief.

3.	A construction cost estimate, which is sufficiently detailed to enable a cost strategy to be devised.

4.	Design Risk Register with any significant hazards/risk that cannot be designed out, etc.

Note: this register derives from the project Risk Assessment and should be kept as a live document throughout the project and updated with any new risks or the removal of those risks that no longer apply due to design being changed, etc.

Sustainability Checkpoint 1

The Handover Strategy has an impact on the assembly of the project team, and the RIBA Plan of Work 2013 encourages the consideration of handover and in-use activities at this stage to ensure that appropriate Schedules of Services are prepared and adequate budgets included in the Project Budget.

Sustainability aims

During Stage 1 the Sustainability Aspirations should be considered and included in the Initial Project Brief, defining criteria to be met as appropriate. A budget, Procurement route and design process should be established that will promote the realisation of those aspirations, and a project team with the required resources, skills and commitment assembled.

Key actions

1.	Confirm that formal sustainability targets, environmental requirements, building lifespan and future climate parameters are stated in the Initial Project Brief.
2.	Check that the principles of the Handover Strategy and post-completion services are included in each consultant's Schedule of Services.
3.	State the internal environmental conditions and formal sustainability targets.
4.	State the building lifespan and future climate parameters.
5.	Undertake early stage consultation, surveys or monitoring as necessary to meet sustainability criteria or assessment procedures.
6.	Define the involvement of the design team after Practical Completion.
7.	Start the Site Waste Management Plan.

	8.	Commission surveys of existing buildings to be retained (including condition, historic/townscape significance, materials and components for recycling), services, noise, vibration, renewable energy resources, ecology, geology, etc as required to inform the brief.
	9.	Review options for formal assessment of aspects of sustainability and/or energy performance (eg BREEAM, LEED, Passivhaus). Establish a timetable for associated assessor appointment and early stage actions.
	10.	Include a simple description in the Initial Project Brief of the internal environmental conditions that the client requires.
	11.	Agree how to measure performance In Use, what incentives there will be to achieve Project Outcomes and what action is appropriate if anything falls short.
	12.	Develop potential energy strategies, including estimated energy demand calculations, options for renewables and implications for building or site design (eg whether there is sufficient plant space).
	13.	Develop water efficiency strategies to establish similarly robust performance targets.
	14.	Set out sustainable drainage systems (SuDS) and surface water retention requirements.
	15.	Develop a brief for any specialist environmental sub-consultants (eg wind monitoring consultants, ecologists).
	16.	Consider climate change adaptation criteria and future performance standards.
	17.	Set out any future uses or reconfiguration to be accommodated.

18.	Ensure that the competence of potential design team members matches the client's Sustainability Aspirations. The team should be balanced, with members of similar competence and commitment and with complimentary contracts of engagement.
19.	Client to implement the Site Waste Management Plan to enable designers to record decisions made to reduce waste as the project progresses.

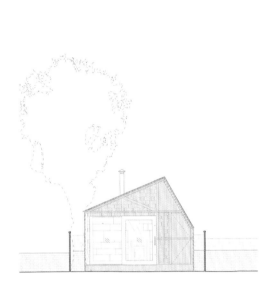

> **Architect:**
> Weston Surman &
> Deane Architecture

Date completed:
April 2013

Construction cost:
£31,000

Awards:
Shortlisted – AJ Small
Projects Award 2014

WSD Architecture were commissioned by an author and illustrator to design and build a 'writer's shed', acting as designer, project manager and lead contractor. The design sought to satisfy the client's need for a functional workspace, but also to create a building that reflected his passion for children's literature and mythologies.

The space is conceived as a haven in the city; a fairy-tale hut at the bottom of the garden where the client can retreat and immerse himself in his work. Externally, the glowing cedar facade, shingle cladding, log store and chimney all play a part in creating this world. Inside, a large north-facing skylight floods the workspace with natural light.

Internally on the gable wall, a bookcase meanders around the wood burning stove, providing a centrepiece for the client to store his library of books. Looking back out over the garden, the glazed sliding door gives way on to a covered verandah – a space perfect for enjoying the very worst of the British weather.

Oiled OSB (oriented strand board) and painted pine tongue and groove were used for the floors, walls and shelving, while utilitarian garden taps and brass splash-backs surround the reclaimed sink. A hearth made of cut concrete paving slabs was built to surround the stove.

Project issues

Surveys

Along with the brief and relevant building sector knowledge, proper inspections and surveys of sites and existing buildings are essential at an early stage; and poor Site Information can lead to problems later. When considering the survey you must establish:

— The kind of survey needed and precisely what is to be surveyed.
— Who will carry out the survey – the architect or a land or building surveyor.
— Who will pay for the survey and where liability will rest in the event of errors.
— The boundaries of the site to be surveyed or the limits of the building.
— That access/keys will be available.

Always heed the RIBA Safety Code for occupied building sites and unoccupied buildings and sites (see below) and refer to the RIBA Chartered Practice Health and Safety Policy Template at www.architecture.com.

Fig. 0.1

RIBA Safety Code

Health and Safety

Health and Safety legislation lays clear obligations on clients, designers, and principal contractors. The following code is complementary advice to all architects engaged in visits to buildings and sites.

Visits to building sites, unoccupied buildings and construction operations can be potentially dangerous. Consider the likely hazards. Follow the safety code.

1 Occupied building sites

The Contractor or occupier has a responsibility for the safety of persons lawfully on site. Do not enter sites or buildings without permission, and immediately report to the person in charge. Comply with all requests from the contractor, his representative or other supervisory staff. See the contractor when you arrive, and when you leave the site.

Wear suitable clothing, in particular protective headgear (a hard hat) and stout shoes or boots. Do not wear thin-soled or slippery shoes. Avoid loose clothes which might catch on an obstruction.

Check that ladders are securely fixed and that planks are secure. Beware of overhead projections, scaffolding and plant, and proceed with caution. Particular care is necessary in windy, cold, wet or muddy conditions. Keep clear of excavations and beware of openings in floors etc. Do not lean on guard rails, scaffoldings etc. Do not interfere with any temporary barriers, guard rails or lights. Beware of ladders on which the rungs may have rusted or rotted, and never climb a ladder which is not securely fixed at the top.

Do not touch any plant or equipment. Keep clear of machinery and stacked materials. Watch out for temporary cables, pumps, hoses and electric fittings.

Do not walk and look around at the same time. Keep one hand free at all times when moving. Make sure that you are in a safe and balanced position whenever making notes or taking photographs.

Report to the contractor anything that comes to your notice on the site as being unsafe.

2 Unoccupied buildings and sites

As a general rule do not visit an empty building or unoccupied site on your own. Make sure someone knows where you are, and at what time you expect to return.

Do not take chances. Do not visit an empty building if you think it unsafe. Do not visit an unoccupied site if you think it dangerous. Anticipate hazards.

Common dangers include:

– the possibility of partial or total structural collapse
– rotten or insecure floors and stairs
– hidden pits, ducts, openings etc, fragile construction, eg asbestos or plastic sheets on roofs
– space which has not been used or ventilated for some time
– live services
– contamination by chemicals or asbestos
– intruders who may still be around
– contamination by vermin or birds, or poisonous substances put down to control them.

Plan the visit and make sure that you take with you appropriate equipment and protective clothing. Apart from stout shoes and a hard hat, remember that unoccupied buildings can be dirty, damp, cold and dark; so go prepared.

Look for defects in the floors ahead, eg wet areas, holes, materials that might be covering up holes.

Familiarise yourself beforehand with the plan of the building, particularly the exit routes. Make sure that security devices on exits will allow you to reach safety quickly.

Walk over the structural members (eg joists, beams, etc) whenever possible - do not rely on floorboards alone.

Do not walk and look around at the same time. Keep one hand free at all times when moving. Do not walk and try to take notes at the same time. Make sure that you are in a safe and balanced position when taking photographs or stretching out to take measurements.

Check on protection when approaching stairwells, lift shafts, roof perimeters, etc.

Do not assume that services (eg cables, sockets, pipes, etc) are safe or have been isolated.

If you suspect the presence of gas, inflammable liquids, dangerous chemicals or free asbestos fibre leave the building immediately.

If you sustain cuts, penetration by nails or other serious injury, seek immediate medical advice.

Always heed these three golden rules:

– do not rush
– if uncertain do not proceed – seek advice or assistance
– do not smoke or use naked flame.

Visual survey checklist

— General context and character, outstanding visual features.
— Any construction work currently under way.
— Traffic movement patterns, noise, pollution.
— Derelict areas, nearby blackspots, visually detracting features.
— Aspect, orientation, shelter, overshadowing from adjacent buildings or trees.
— Properties adjoining the site, their condition, usage, evidence of subsidence, fire risks, party walls, etc.
— Possible health and safety hazards.
— Adjacent waterways, railways, busy roads.
— Possible restrictions on site access, delivery or site working.
— Possible restrictions due to sensitive building uses adjacent, eg hospital, nursery school, law court.

Site survey information

The information presented in the survey plans and reports might be expected to include the following:
— Site boundary.
— Outline of existing buildings.
— Boundary fences, access ways, garden and adjacent walls; their height, profile, material, ownership and condition.
— Ditches, ponds, waterways above or below ground.
— Rights of way/access (check with client's solicitors, local authority).
— Spot levels at appropriate intervals, plus:
—— Services covers, etc.
—— Pavement kerbs and road crowns where they enter the site.
—— Indicate all services above and below ground adjacent to, connecting into or crossing the site with relevant levels, falls, heights, access points, manholes (show cover levels and inverts).
— Pylons, posts (show headroom).
— Soil and surface water drains.
— Water mains.

— Electricity cables.
— Telecommunication cables.
— Gas mains.
— Any other services.
— Trees, hedges and large shrubs, their height and position, spread of branches and diameter of trunk 1 metre above ground level.

Surveys of existing buildings

The measured survey drawings might show:
— Plans, sections, elevations.
— Elevational features, eg plinths, string courses, openings.
— Precise levels at floors, datum, thickness and construction.
— Levels of external ground.

A written report might include information that cannot be shown graphically, such as:
— Structural and other defects and their causes.
— Dry rot, damp penetration, condensation.
— Infestation by rodents, beetles and other insects.
— Recent repairs and decoration.
— Settlement cracks, misshapen openings, gaps at skirtings and windows.
— Walls that are misaligned or have bulges.
— Sagging roofs, defective roof coverings.
— Deflection of beams or lintels; cracks at beam bearings.

The architects/surveyors should state whether or not they were able to see inside the structure of the building and how much they were able to see. It is important not to infer the state of the whole building from sight of one part of it.

Where appropriate, the client should be advised to call in specialists in particular areas, eg mechanical, electrical, timber treatment.

A statement on the following lines should appear at the end of the relevant part of the report (as stipulated in most PI insurance policies):

It has not been possible to make a detailed examination of the floor or roof construction except at the positions described because material damage would have been caused in gaining access. It is therefore impossible to make any statement about the condition of the unexamined structure.

Developing the brief

The brief should be developed alongside the emerging design in three stages with increasing levels of detail:

Stage 0 –	Strategic Brief
Stage 1 –	Initial Project Brief
Stage 2 –	Final Project Brief

Strategic Brief
The Strategic Brief should clearly state the client's objectives and what they wish to achieve with the project. It will refer to functional requirements, environmental standards, level of quality, lifespan and maintenance and should be seen as the basis for Feasibility Studies. It should also outline the sort of decisions that need to be made and who will be the key decision makers in the process.

Initial Project Brief
The Initial Project Brief will cover the technical, managerial and design intentions, and shows how these requirements are to be met. It will be based on a number of sources, including the Feasibility Studies; site or building survey and studies; research into functional needs; environmental considerations; statutory constraints and construction cost estimate.

Final Project Brief
The Final Project Brief should further define the design requirements and should be signed off by the client after approval at the end of Stage 2. Any subsequent changes should be recorded, identifying their impact on the project and architect's services, and formally agreed with the client.

Client-led changes can be a key factor in reducing profit margin, and recording change is therefore a critical activity. It may not be possible to agree additional fees for all changes but if after a while they become significant, having a record of them will be invaluable in the negotiation process. Beware of 'commission creep' and note that the RIBA appointments include provisions for the charging of additional fees where additional work is instructed.

Refer to Stage 2: Managing project-related change.

Project brief pro forma

General

This checklist can be used to develop the brief across all three stages:

1.	Project Objectives – a 'mission statement' including the context of the project, overall scope and purpose, client's objectives, requirements and priorities and what is expected in response to the brief.
2.	How the success of the project will be measured.
3.	Statement on image and quality.
4.	Client's organisational structure and function (where appropriate) and spatial relationships.
5.	Target programme, including any phasing.
6.	Statements on size and capacity requirements and functions to be accommodated.
7.	Technology to be incorporated or accommodated, including equipment, services and IT.
8.	Quality requirements for materials, construction and long-term maintenance.
9.	Key targets for quality, time and cost, including milestones for decisions.
10.	Life expectancy of building and components, flexibility to accommodate future reorganisation, allowance for future expansion or extension.
11.	User's considerations (where this is not the client).
12.	Health and safety policy.
13.	Functional requirements of direct client/user client.
14.	Preferred spatial relationships.
15.	Agreed project BIM protocols (if appropriate).
16.	Procurement process.
17.	Method for assessing and managing risks and validating design proposals.
18.	Outline specifications of general and specific areas.
19.	Servicing options and specification implications, eg security, deliveries, access, workplace.

Site

1.	Likelihood of archaeological discoveries.
2.	Known development plans for surrounding area.
3.	Leasehold/freehold interests and party walls, rights of light, access or other known easements.

4.   Site constraints (physical and legal), opportunities, etc.

5.   Site history, topography and geology.

6.   Exact location of boundaries.

7.   Services below ground and known restrictions on development.

8.   Known problems with the site, eg geological conditions, hazardous substances, presence of contaminated land.

9.   Known problems with existing building, eg presence of asbestos.

Planning and building considerations

1.   Statutory requirements.

2.   Known constraints arising from previous consents or conditions.

3.   Likelihood of planning gain or Section 106 agreement.

4.   Impact of the local development plan.

5.   Statutory or agreed space standards.

6.   Other stakeholders, eg English Heritage.

7.   Likely parking requirements.

8.   Access requirements, including disabled access.

Environmental

1.   Client's environmental policy (if appropriate).

2.   Internal and external environmental requirements.

3.   Operational and maintenance requirements.

4.   Options for environmental control.

Financial

1.   Capital expenditure budget and cash flow constraints.

2.   Approximate cost per square metre.

3.   Grants, subsidies or information relating to tax advantages, eg VAT.

4.   Budget for all elements.

5.   Targets and constraints on operating expenditure and other whole-life costs.

Project strategies (to be developed from Stage 2 onwards)

1.	Technology (ie IT and BIM).
2.	Communication.
3.	Building Control.
4.	Procurement.
5.	Construction.
6.	Handover.
7.	Maintenance and Operation.
8.	Sustainability.
9.	Health and Safety.

Refer to Stage 2 in Guide to using the RIBA Plan of Work 2013 *for advice on Project Strategies.*

The RIBA has produced a Briefing and Evaluation Toolkit which can be accessed by RIBA members through www.architecture.com

Project programming

Project overruns are frequently the source of a reduced profit margin and it is essential that you plan resource needs when preparing the fee proposal and then monitor them at least weekly. It can be difficult to assess progress on the initial stages where the design process is iterative but regardless of the work stage you should set out all the activities into a simple Gantt chart that follows the timescales set out in your proposal. Follow the advice set out in 'Stage 1: Lean thinking and creating value' to help manage waste in the design process. A format for resource planning and monitoring spreadsheets can be found in the *RIBA Handbook of Practice Management 9th edition* (2013), and these are also available from www.ribabookshops.com/SPH.

 The programme is a key tool and should be referred to regularly throughout the project.

Use the programme to assess in-house resource requirements and the overall duration of each stage in the design process. It can then be used to measure progress, particularly if activities are linked and a critical path set out as a result. It can also be linked to other project team members' programmes, and where the design team is working collaboratively, a single, integrated Project Programme can be developed.

Should the activities slip, the appropriate action should be taken to put it right, such as increasing personnel. This will obviously have an effect on the project's cash flow so make sure this is managed as well. Ultimately however, if a project starts to slip you will need to find out if the client will accept a slip in the programme and if not you will need to agree measures to bring it back on track. There will be occasions when slippage is due to matters outside your control or variations to the brief, in which case you will need to agree an extension to the Design Programme and, if appropriate, additional fees.

The programme can start as a 'high-level' strategic tool with more detail added as the project progresses. The contractor will of course be responsible for maintaining and managing the Construction Programme during Stage 5. A simple programme can be created in MS Excel or, for more sophisticated programmes providing critical path analysis, MS Project can be used. For advice on programming refer to *Programming and Scheduling Techniques* (Thomas Uher and Adam S Zantis, 2011) and *Construction Planning Programming and Control: 3rd edition* (B Nutt, 2009).

Lean thinking and creating value

One of the key areas where time can be wasted is in the design process. Whilst it is important to explore all the options at the beginning and determine the one that best meets the brief and the client's aspirations, developing options in detail that are later dropped does not add value. Instead the aim should be to progressively fix the design, obviating the need to revisit decisions made in earlier design stages.

This can be achieved by following these guidelines:

1. **Don't start designing until you're ready**
    Have the necessary information with respect to the brief, the site and all necessary knowledge of the sector (eg residential, retail, etc) and the pertinent regulations, planning constraints, etc before you put pen to paper.

2. **Establish your design agenda**
    Know what you want to achieve in terms of quality, cost, marketing value (from the practice's point of view), etc and of course the ambitions of the client. For example, are you prepared to spend more time (and generate less profit) because the building has high marketing potential for the practice?

3. **Undertake design activities collaboratively**
    See below for advice on optimising the value of design workshops.

4. **Use your expertise**
    Ensure that the people with the best knowledge on a given matter are involved in all key design decisions.

5. **Don't change what you have fixed**
    Use progressive fixity and avoid revisiting decisions made during a previous design stage.

Design workshops

Rather than auditing design output after it has been developed (and potentially having to take corrective action), ensure that the design work is properly informed at the beginning through collaborative design workshops. These can provide an environment in which all the knowledge necessary for the specific design activity can be located in one place. To derive the most benefit from the workshop, it is important that design is actually undertaken there rather than it merely being a place to collate data to be used in the design. Having those with the best knowledge sitting around the table will ensure that the best expertise available within the practice is applied:

— To every project.
— At the right times in the project cycle.
— In the most effective way possible.

This can feel a somewhat counter-intuitive design methodology. Architects' training involves working largely on their own and evaluating their solutions through critical review by peers, after the design stage has been completed. To work effectively the knowledge-led design process needs to be part of the ethos of each individual and used consistently.

Tips on brainstorming

There are four basic rules in brainstorming. These are intended to reduce social inhibitions among group numbers, stimulate idea generation and increase overall creativity of the group.

1. **Focus on quantity**
   This is a means of enhancing divergent production, aiming to facilitate problem solving through the maxim 'quantity breeds quality'. The assumption is that the greater the number of ideas generated, the greater the chance of producing a radical and effective solution.

2. **Withhold criticism**
   In brainstorming criticism of ideas generated should be put on hold. Instead participants should focus on extending or adding to ideas, reserving criticism for a later 'critical' stage of the process. By suspending judgement participants will feel free to generate unusual ideas.

3. **Welcome unusual ideas**
   Unusual ideas can be generated by looking from new perspectives and suspending assumptions. These new ways of thinking may provide better solutions.

4. **Combine and improve ideas**
   Good ideas may be combined to form a single, better idea. This can stimulate the building of ideas by a process of association (ie the experience of a stimulus leading to the effects of another due to repeated pairing).

Knowledge-leaders

Establish knowledge-leaders – individuals within the practice with recognised skills and expertise in certain fields, which might include creative design, sustainable design, technical design and the principal sectors you operate in, such as residential, retail, etc.

These individuals should have the responsibility of maintaining and developing knowledge in their field and injecting it into the project design process through the design workshops. Once appointed to a project, a knowledge-leader should remain involved with it through to completion.

For micro practices this goal might be achieved through knowledge-sharing and collaboration with other practices or individuals who have complementary experience.

A brief note about 'value'

Knowledge Management facilitates continuous improvement, a cornerstone of the lean design principles that originated in the motor industry. Lean thinking is focused on efficiency and the elimination of waste, and is based on five principles:

Specify what creates value from the customer's perspective.
Identify all steps across the whole value stream.
Make the activities flow.
Only produce what is pulled (needed) by the customer on a just-in-time basis.
Strive for perfection by continually removing successive layers of waste.

For an explanation of these points and more advice on lean design in the construction industry you can refer to www.leanconstruction.org or www.lci.uk.org.

S18

Graticule Architecture were asked to design a temporary space to hold a series of performance pieces by an artist client, Rosie Jackson. The brief set out the requirement for a fully demountable house-like shelter of roughly 35m² that would provide the setting for an ever-evolving performance piece. The artist hoped that the structure would become integral to the performance, acting as both prop and shelter, and that it could be reconstructed at different locations, in different arrangements.

In the summer of 2012, conscious of the limited budget of £6,000, Graticule Architecture set out to design value into low-cost, readily available material. A kit of parts, the Rope House consists of three primary materials. The structure was assembled from Key Clamp components and lengths of galvanised scaffolding poles. On to this 'dumb' structure precisely designed Perspex spacers would be attached to offset the 5km length of spliced rope. Conceptually the building begins as a fraying cord some way away from the structure, leading to the site. When the rope meets the foot of the building it begins to wrap the structure – in turn providing wall, floor and roof – and is kept in tension by a weighed spool hanging from the apex of the structure.

With both directors of Graticule Architecture affiliated with universities, they also saw the project as a means of providing valuable on-site experience to their students. Rope House would become a case study in the dialogue between digital design processes and traditional craft techniques. It also came to demonstrate the value that design can bring to a project. In its component parts, Rope House has very limited value – through design the whole really is greater than the sum of its parts.

Practice issues

Financial management

While making money is not the reason most architects go into practice, poor financial control is often the reason they go out of business. Profit is essential as it ensures that the practice will continue to exist and grow in the future, and sound financial management, particularly with respect to collection of fees, is of fundamental importance.

A practice's financial management system should include the following:

— A long-term plan setting out ambitions and targets.
— An annual business plan budget setting out anticipated income, expenditure and profit. Once set, this should not be altered, but should be used as a benchmark to monitor against during the year ahead.
— Shorter-term, usually monthly but more frequently if circumstances demand, forecasts of income, expenditure and profit.
— A project-based system for forecasting and monitoring resource needs and other project costs.
— Monthly management accounts reporting performance against the budget and forecasts.
— A system of ledgers and timesheets to record invoices issued, cash collected, time spent, supplier invoices received, and other expenditure.

It is now more important than ever to run a tight ship and manage cash flow through the business. These are some of the more important matters to bear in mind:

— Plan annual expenditure 'bottom up', by assessing needs and then checking affordability against projected income and profit. If the sums don't add up assess priorities and adjust the plan accordingly.
— Distinguish between invoices that are 100% secure, have a signed appointment and an agreed programme, and those that retain elements of risk. Assess the risk and allocate a cost that reflects that. For example, if a project is reckoned to have a 50% chance of proceeding, put half of the fee income into the forecast.
— Produce a monthly management account to show performance against the annual budget and the previous month's forecast in terms of income, cost and profit. Keep it simple and use it to spot trends and as an aid to plan additional/reduced spending as well as simply monitoring and recording performance. To work properly, this activity requires regular input of income, expenditure and time records.
— Closely monitor cash collection and deal with late payment as a top priority.

— Make sure invoices are sent out as soon as possible in line with the appointment and agreed cash flow. The invoice should clearly set out what it relates to, how much has been paid previously, what is being invoiced at this time, and, if relevant, the VAT payment (make sure to include the practice's VAT number). Either the invoice itself or the covering letter should confirm any preferred payment methods and the timetable for settlement. You should then send reminders for accounts that have not been settled on time.

— A spreadsheet can be set up using fixed percentages to cover the prevailing rate of employer's National Insurance contribution, overhead allowance and 'productivity factor' (the percentage of the full potential working year that an individual is likely to spend on income-producing work, excluding holiday and an allowance for sickness and working on administration or other non-income-producing work). 'Other employment costs' (pension contribution, other insurances, car allowances, etc) and profit percentages (to calculate charge-out rates) need to be established on an individual basis. As noted above, this calculation can be done either by individual or by grade of staff. In the latter case it will be necessary to establish average figures for the grade in question.

The practice will need to calculate its overhead cost allowing for all non-productive costs (including such things as rent, rates, insurances, administrative staff, marketing, business development, etc), and establish how to apportion these to the individual or grade rates. The RIBA *Good Practice Guide: Painless Financial Management* provides more detail on how to work out these rates, based on the method excluding overheads. Once this is done, a resource-based fee projection should be established by estimating the number of staff that will be needed to provide the required services on the project, and the number of person hours needed at each stage. This, multiplied by their hourly rates, will produce the estimated cost to the practice of undertaking the project and thus inform the fee sought.

VAT and small practices

Most practices are limited companies, and it is sensible for small practices to incorporate as well. For micro practices, particularly sole practitioners, you can decide whether or not to register for VAT. Strictly speaking it is only necessary to register if the company's annual earnings are over HMRC's prescribed threshold (currently £81,000), although practitioners may choose to register regardless of anticipated income, to project the image of a larger business. If the intention is to take on larger commercial projects, clients will generally expect to pay VAT and not charging it may not necessarily be a benefit to them. This approach would not suit a practice intending to work on house extensions and other similar-sized projects, however, where the increase in cost might make them uncompetitive against other small practices. The set-up can be changed relatively easily but this should be part of the initial business-planning process. If the business is VAT registered it can be set up on a flat rate. For architects this means only paying 14.5% of the gross figure (ie the fee + VAT amount). This figure is reduced to 13.5% in the first year of trading. This reduces the administration required but expenses cannot then be off-set separately as they are considered to be subsumed within the lower rate. You should check the current arrangement on www.hmrc.gov.uk.

Refer to the RIBA *Handbook of Practice Management 9th edition* (2013) and the RIBA Fees Calculator (available through the members' area of www.architecture.com) for further financial advice.

> Stage summary

A key theme of this book is making a reasonable profit out of small projects, something that many small practices struggle to do. Efficiency is of course at the core of this aim and depends on getting started and setting up the project in the right way. That means:

— Not starting until you are ready, ie having all the necessary information on the following:
—— Site.
—— Building type.
—— Relevant regulations.
—— Planning context.
— Having a properly researched and considered, written brief.
— Establishing the precise scope of work to be undertaken and the programme, with key milestones identified.
— Setting this understanding out in an appointment and making sure the client is fully aware of:
—— The skills you will be bringing and their value.
—— The implications of making changes to the brief.

 Managing your client's expectations is a key skill necessary for successful practice.

Once Stage 1 has been completed you should have agreed a preferred, single development option and have the information necessary to develop the design in the usual, iterative manner but with risk properly managed and the way open to a successful project.

Section II

Progressive Fixity

Introduction

Stages 2 and 3 will build on the foundations of work undertaken in Stages 0 and 1 (learning from Stage 7 activities on previous projects). The design will become more tangible as it takes shape. You will need to communicate clearly to the client, particularly one who is inexperienced in reading architectural drawings, and ensure that the drawings and images you produce properly reflect the end product.

Stages 2 and 3 represent the creative design stage of a project and for many are therefore the most rewarding (along with seeing your creation become reality on site). However, it can also be the stage at which wasted effort is at its highest. During Stages 2 and 3 the design process generally proceeds in a non-linear fashion, where it is hardest to use the principle of 'progressive fixity'. However, to make the process as efficient as possible – and therefore keep profit level as high as possible – the aim should be to keep waste to a minimum, and this section contains advice on how to achieve that.

Stages 2 and 3 have been grouped together, reflecting:

— The iterative nature of design during this phase of the project.
— The fact that for small projects, the planning process is generally (but not always) more compact, with less supporting information required.

Some clients will want the planning application processed at an early stage to keep costs low. It is important to explain the potential pitfalls and 'false economy' of such an approach.

This issue has been acknowledged in the Plan of Work by having Town Planning set out as a 'variable' task bar.

Stage 2

Concept Design

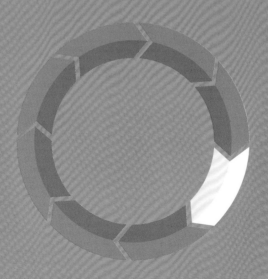

RIBA Plan of Work 2013 Stage 2

RIBA
Plan of
Work
2013

Stage 2

Concept Design

Task Bar	Tasks
Core Objectives	Prepare **Concept Design**, including outline proposals for structural design, building services systems, outline specifications and preliminary **Cost Information** along with relevant **Project Strategies** in accordance with **Design Programme**. Agree alterations to brief and issue **Final Project Brief**.
Procurement *Variable task bar*	*The Procurement activities during this stage will depend on the procurement route determined during Stage 1.*
Programme *Variable task bar*	Review **Project Programme**.
(Town) Planning *Variable task bar*	*The RIBA Plan of Work 2013 enables planning applications to be submitted at the end of Stage 2. However, this is not the anticipated norm, but rather an option to be exercised only in response to a specific client's needs and with due regard to the associated risks.*
Suggested Key Support Tasks	Prepare **Sustainability Strategy**, **Maintenance** and **Operational Strategy** and review **Handover Strategy** and **Risk Assessments**. Undertake third party consultations as required and any **Research and Development** aspects. Review and update **Project Execution Plan**. Consider **Construction Strategy**, including offsite fabrication, and develop **Health and Safety Strategy**. *During this stage a number of strategies that complement the design are prepared. These strategies consider post-occupancy and operational issues along with the consideration of buildability. Third party consultations are also essential.*
Sustainability Checkpoints	• *Confirm that formal sustainability pre-assessment and identification of key areas of design focus have been undertaken and that any deviation from the* **Sustainability Aspirations** *has been reported and agreed.* • *Has the initial Building Regulations Part L assessment been carried out?* • *Have 'plain English' descriptions of internal environmental conditions and seasonal control strategies and systems been prepared?* • *Has the environmental impact of key materials and the* **Construction Strategy** *been checked?* • *Has resilience to future changes in climate been considered?*
Information Exchanges (at stage completion)	**Concept Design** including outline structural and building services design, associated **Project Strategies**, preliminary **Cost Information** and **Final Project Brief**.
UK Government Information Exchanges	Required.

Introduction

Stage 2 maps exactly to the former Stage C.

The stage involves:

— Producing the Concept Design in line with the Initial Project Brief.
— Developing the Project Strategies, such as those for sustainability, maintenance and operation, risk and construction.
— Developing the Initial Project Brief into the Final Project Brief.
— Updating the Project Execution Plan as necessary.
— Developing the cost plan in tandem with the design. This may be undertaken by a cost consultant, but on small projects where one has not been appointed, a less formal process should still be undertaken. This section provides information to facilitate that activity.

If a pre-application planning submission is to be made it is likely that it will be at this stage, and there is advice on this below.

 The client should be made aware that any changes after sign-off of the Final Project Brief will very likely have an impact on the cost and programme of the design process.

Project activities

Information required

1.	Initial Project Brief.
2.	Feasibility Studies.
3.	Stage 1 report.
4.	Construction cost estimate.
5.	Relevant technical data, trade information, regulations, standards, planning policies, etc.
6.	If relevant, BIM protocols.

Stage activities

1.	Check you have all the information you need from the client and request anything that is missing.
2.	Check that the Initial Project Brief has been signed off by the client, and develop it into the Final Project Brief by the end of the stage.

Evaluate the content of the brief to establish that:

— It reflects the client's stated objectives.
— It provides an adequate basis for design.
— The time and cost parameters are reasonable.
— All the information the client should provide before design commences is provided.

If changes to the brief are necessary, make sure that these are subject to the Change Control Procedures established in the Project Plan.

Refer to Stage 2: Project plan pro forma.

| 3. | Advise the client on the need to appoint further consultants and specialists. |

Decisions may be needed for the Concept Design which require specialist advice on structure, services, environmental and other matters.

| 4. | Advise the client on health and safety matters. |

Refer to Stage 0: CDM responsibilities (for clients).

| 5. | Advise the client if the project requires listed building or conservation area consent, and action accordingly. You should be able to identify listed and 'locally listed' buildings and conservation areas on the local authority's website. |

Refer to the English Heritage website for advice on how to make a listed building consent application:
www.english-heritage.org.uk/professional/advice/our-planning-role/consent/lbc

Refer also to the Planning Portal:
www.planningportal.gov.uk/permission/responsibilities/beforeyoustart/
otherpermissions/listed

| 6. | Prepare the Project Strategies. |

With regard to the Procurement and Construction Strategies, review the options for Procurement with the client and note any matters which could affect the choice of Procurement route. In particular it is important to identify who will be carrying out any specialist areas of design, for example whether they will be handled by the design team or by specialist subcontractors. This has implications for the consultants' terms of appointment, liability and warranty arrangements as well as affecting the Procurement route to be adopted.

| 7. | Prepare the Handover Strategy. |

The Handover Strategy includes the requirements for phased handovers, commissioning, training of staff and other factors crucial to the successful occupation of a building.

On some projects, the Building Services Research and Information Association (BSRIA) Soft Landings process is used as the basis for formulating the strategy and undertaking Post-occupancy Evaluations. Refer to www.bsria.co.uk/services/design/soft-landings.

Refer to the Post-occupancy Evaluation (POE) activities listed under Stage 6.

| 8. | Agree input to the stage by design team members. |

Refer to the Design Responsibility Matrix in the RIBA Plan of Work 2013 Toolkit available free at www. ribaplanofwork.com.

Remind design team members to identify current legislation (eg Building Regulations, health and safety legislation) with which the project must conform.

Discuss with design team members the performance standards, environmental provisions and budget allocation required to comply with the brief.

| 9. | Check the scope of professional services agreed between the client and other consultants to ensure there are no gaps in the services. |

Refer to Stage 2: Risk management.

| 10. | Check the Stage 2/3 timetable against the agreed project timetable. The timetable should show critical points by which information from the client and design team members will be required. It should also show key milestones for review of design health and safety issues. |

11.	Confirm the programme and pattern for design team meetings.

12.	If a BIM protocol is to be followed and you have been appointed as information manager: — Organise a BIM pre-start meeting. — Organise initial model sharing with the design team for strategic analysis and options appraisal. — Identify key model elements such as prefabricated components, and create concept-level parametric objects for all major elements. — Enable design team access to BIM data. — Agree extent of performance specified work. — Assist members of the design team to develop the design using the BIM model, ensuring that data-sharing protocols are followed. — Check and sign off the model at agreed stages. — Issue or assist in the issue of design data at agreed times throughout the development of the design. — Assist in the development of data relative to the agreed levels of detail. — Assist in the integration of contractor's, subcontractors' and suppliers' data into the BIM model.

13.	If it is part of your scope of work, check with relevant authorities concerning highways, drainage, water, gas and electricity, etc and requirements for plant and meter housings, substations, etc. Check whether bodies such as the Environment Agency will have an interest in the development, and if so consult with them as appropriate.

14.	It may be appropriate to view similar projects elsewhere with the client. Check they are happy with any expenditure associated with this exercise before making arrangements. Appraise and analyse the schemes.

15.	Prepare the Concept Design, including outline proposals for structural design, services systems, landscape, outline specifications and preliminary Cost Information along with relevant Project Strategies.

16.	Advise the client about any proposals to introduce innovative design or construction ideas or the specifying of relatively new materials, and ask the client to confirm awareness of these in writing.
17.	Explain to the client the benefits of submitting a pre-application submission and, if this strategy is agreed, prepare and submit the necessary drawings and other information. *Refer to Stage 2: Standard layout for pre-application submissions.* *Refer to* Town Planning: RIBA Plan of Work 2013 Guide *(2014) for detailed advice on the planning process, and also to the UK government website www.planningportal.gov.uk.*
18.	Review the Maintenance and Operational Strategy and the Health and Safety Strategy and update the project plan accordingly. This should be carried out in conjunction with the client and the principal designer.
19.	Establish whether notices under the Party Wall etc Act 1996 will be needed.
20.	If a principal designer has been appointed, work with him/her and all other designers in carrying out Risk Assessments and in drafting the pre-construction information.
21.	Review the Cost Information. Provide information to the cost consultant for the initial cost plan and cash flow projection (or prepare an approximation of construction cost if appointed to do so).
22.	Prepare a Stage 2 report which should include drawings, decisions reached, the Final Project Brief, Project Programme, Project Objectives and Strategies and any response received from the local authority planning officer on a pre-app submission.

Information exchange

1.	Final Project Brief.
2.	Concept Design.
	This should show the design sufficiently developed for the client to understand, comment on and approve the proposals. It may be appropriate to make simple models or produce 3D sketch views to assist with this.
	The design should include outline structural and mechanical services design (usually prepared by the engineers).
	It should also include the construction and environmental methods proposed.
3.	Project Strategies.
	Refer to Stage 2: Project plan pro-forma for possible contents.
4.	Preliminary Cost Information.
5.	Preliminary Risk Register to be issued to Design Team, Client and principal designer and Initial Pre-Construction Information content to be passed to principal designer.
6.	Potentially a pre-application planning submission.
7.	Stage 2 report.

Sustainability Checkpoint 2

Sustainability aims

To develop a Concept Design that embodies the Sustainability Aspirations of the project with sufficient detail and analysis to be confident that key strategies can be delivered in practice.

Key actions

1.	Undertake formal sustainability pre-assessment and identification of key areas of design focus.
2.	Report on deviation from aspirations.
3.	Undertake initial Approved Document L assessment.
4.	Prepare a 'plain English' description of internal environmental conditions, seasonal control strategy and systems.
5.	Check the environmental impact of key materials and the Construction Strategy.
6.	Consider resilience to future changes in climate.
7.	Set out the site-scale environmental design criteria (eg solar orientation, overshadowing, SuDS, waste).
8.	Establish maximum plan depths to achieve desired levels of natural ventilation, daylight and view.
9.	Design for buildability, usability and manageability.
10.	Consider the impact of complexity of form on thermal performance, airtightness and inefficient or wasteful use of materials.

11.	Establish an appropriate glazing proportion and shading strategy for each orientation to provide good levels of daylight while avoiding excessive glare, solar gain or heat loss.
12.	Establish appropriate element thicknesses to achieve the U-values required by the energy strategy.
13.	Check that materials and the construction approach will provide a level of thermal mass that is appropriate to the environmental design strategy.
14.	Refine and review design decisions to minimise the quantity of materials used and to minimise construction waste (for guidance, see www.wrap.org.uk/designingoutwaste).
15.	Review the embodied impacts of the materials and the construction approach in the context of the building's lifespan.
16.	Avoid design solutions that inhibit adaptation and alternative use of the building or its components and materials.
17.	Take particular care to avoid short- and long-term damage to traditional building fabric from ill-considered upgrade interventions.
18.	Ensure that the design implications of any components essential to the success of the Sustainability Strategy (eg space for fuel deliveries and waste handling, roof collector area and orientation, location and size of rainwater harvesting tanks, SuDS attenuation, etc) are understood by all members of the project team.
19.	Refine the energy and servicing strategy, incorporating energy-efficient services design and design techniques.
20.	Carry out sufficient compliance or advanced modelling to prove the design concept before freezing the design (eg SBEM/SAP/PHPP (Passivhaus Planning Package) or dynamic modelling).
21.	Audit the emerging design against the project's Sustainability Strategy and Project Outcomes.
22.	Set up a programme of intermediate evaluations and reality checks involving stakeholders and key users as well as the design team.

Before

After

Architect:
Neil Dusheiko Architects

Date completed:
2013

Construction cost:
£260,000

Awards:
Shortlisted – NLA's Don't Move, Improve! Awards 2013

The client's brief called for a sizeable amount of glazing with large skylights to let light into the depth of the house and glazed doors to provide a link with the outside. A balance needed to be struck between large areas of glazing and improving the overall energy efficiency of the house, which had no insulation at all.

The existing house was in a rundown state and needed considerable repair. The previous owners had removed the original traditional Victorian bay window from the front facade without putting adequate structural support in place, resulting in the facade bowing outwards. The traditional Victorian sash windows had been removed and a mixture of steel and u-PVC windows had been installed, disrupting the historic pattern of windows to the front and rear facades.

The architects met the planning officer on site during the pre-planning application stage to discuss the issue of demolishing the entire rear facade and creating a contemporary glazed extension, which could be clad in an insulated render. They also discussed repairing the bowed front facade and cladding it in insulated render.

The clients agreed to rebuild the traditional bay window to the front facade and re-instate sash windows to the rear, re-establishing the traditional pattern of fenestration to the terrace.

The rationale behind these negotiations was to increase the overall thermal efficiency of the existing building to allow the large amounts of glazed areas towards the rear of the house which faced south. The local authority was supportive of this approach and the plans were passed in eight weeks and the material detail of the facade included as a planning condition.

Project issues

Efficient design processes

One of the core messages of this book is that cutting corners generally leads to increased time and cost in the long run. This extends not just to practice management procedures but to project design development. If you use BIM protocols and the collaborative project team is brought together early in the design process (say from the start of Stage 2) it is likely that you will develop a well-considered and coordinated design. For small projects, input from other consultants (eg cost and engineering) does not have to be significant in the early stages, but as the saying goes 'a stitch in time saves nine'. The client will need to balance the planning risk against the level of involvement of the consultant team that they consider appropriate, and this is an area the architect can advise on. As with many such decisions, think: 'what would I do if I was the client and it was my money being invested'?

One factor in maintaining an efficient design process (and thereby turning a profit) is to give the client the means to make informed decisions about the design and stick to them.

Provide a spread of high-level design proposals in Stage 1 that cover the principal options so that other ideas don't arise later on once the design has been further developed. When a single preferred option has been identified, progressively develop the design in such a way that – as far as possible – you do not need to revisit decisions made earlier and therefore have to discard work previously carried out. Refer to the advice in Stage 1: Lean thinking and creating value.

Managing project-related change

Change can be (and often is) a significant factor in reducing profit from fees. It, and the client's expectations regarding your scope of work, should therefore be carefully managed.

— Follow the guidance set out under Stage 0: Fee proposals and appointments.
— Report regularly to the client on fees and expenses incurred, and submit accounts at agreed intervals.
— Check that the client settles all accounts promptly. Refer to the *Handbook of Practice Management, 9th edition* (2013), Chapter 7 Financial Management, and to the RIBA *Good Practice Guide: Fee Management* (2012). See also Stage 1: Financial management.
— Keep careful records of all conversations, consultations and design team meetings. File all notes and sketches prepared during the design process.
— Report to the client on project cost matters at agreed intervals.
— Alert the client to any matters raised during discussions with statutory or other bodies which might affect the proposals. Explain the implications and discuss what actions should be taken.
— Alert the client to the design implications arising out of health and safety legislation (eg circulation, design of workstations, environmental comfort) and implications for future maintenance, repair and replacement.
— Check that all information requested from the client concerning the site or existing buildings has been supplied.
— Use the 'Design change notice and record' which can be downloaded from www.ribabookshops.com/SPH.

Standard layout for pre-application submissions

Planning pre-application has become more-or-less standard for most projects but there is no firm pre-determined requirement for what is to be submitted. The more information you can provide, the more detailed Feedback the planning officer will be able to give, but if you are uncertain of the outcome you may wish to provide less detailed information first time round and keep the submission at a higher level, but perhaps encompassing a range of design options. This must be tempered to some extent by whether there is a fee to be paid to the local authority, the amount of which can vary from one to another. Increasingly though, planning authorities do require payment before they will give you Feedback.

Pre-application advice will provide you with the planning officer's considered view but cannot of course give certainty as to the outcome of a planning application, which may be subject to other considerations not covered in the pre-application and potentially to a different view held by the Planning Committee.

Some authorities have a standard form to complete but a sensible format for most submissions is an A3 brochure (which can accompany the form) containing the following information:

1. **Introduction:**
   - *a.* Scope of the project.
   - *b.* Project team members and principal contact.
   - *c.* Summary of Feedback requested from the planning officer.

2. **Location Analysis:**
   - *a.* Location plan, annotated to show relevant site issues.
   - *b.* Planning policy context.
   - *c.* Surrounding building uses.
   - *d.* Public transport.

3. **Site Analysis:**
   - *a.* Site plan as existing, annotated with relevant matters.
   - *b.* Street views (photos) of site as existing.
   - *c.* Existing building plans, sections, elevations.
   - *d.* Existing underground and overground services.
   - *e.* Public rights of way.

4. **Design Proposals:**
   - *a.* Client brief.
   - *b.* Options (if appropriate); with the following information for each one:
     - *i.* Proposed plans, sections, elevations.
     - *ii.* Precedent images (if appropriate).
     - *iii.* Environmental sustainability considerations.
     - *iv.* Affordable housing (if relevant).
     - *v.* Transport and servicing issues.
     - *vi.* Noise issues.
     - *vii.* Air quality issues.
     - *viii.* Daylight/sunlight issues (if relevant).
     - *ix.* Area Schedule (existing and proposed).
     - *x.* 3D visualisations (if appropriate).

Project plan pro forma

The project plan (or Quality Plan or Project Execution Plan) is a vital tool in managing the project and keeping a record of progress, and is at the core of most Quality Assurance programmes. It should have a summary page with information on the project and project team:

Job no:
Job title:
Building type:
Estimated value:
Client:
Project director:
Project leader:
Revision/date/notes/date of next review:

It should also set out contact details for companies and key members of the whole project team and the project stakeholders, eg local authority personnel, etc.

It should set out the Project Strategies for:

Technology (ie IT and BIM)
Communication
Building Control
Procurement
Construction
Handover
Maintenance and Operation
Sustainability

These matters should be outlined at Stage 2 and prepared in detail at Stage 3. For advice on what the strategies should contain, refer to *Guide to Using the RIBA Plan of Work 2013.*

The project plan should also cover:

Client brief including any schedules of accommodation, cost plan parameters, target programme, any key constraints, agreed level of specification/cost/durability.

Scope of services to be provided by the architect (under RIBA Plan of Work 2013 stages).

Scope of services to be provided by other consultants (use the Design Responsibility Matrix at www.ribaplanofwork.com).

Change Control Procedures (see Stage 2: Managing project-related change).

Change control records (to be added as project progresses as appropriate).

Project Objectives.

Project Outcomes.

Project Programme.

Record of any client complaints and the resulting corrective action.

For more advice on Project Objectives and Project Outcomes refer to *Guide to using the RIBA Plan of Work 2013*. For advice on programming refer to Stage 1: Project programming.

All these matters should be communicated to the whole project team and agreed and signed off by everyone.

The plan itself should be set out chronologically by RIBA work stage. The downloadable version of this book can form the action checklist, edited as necessary.

If the plan is updated regularly it will provide a snapshot of and a look-ahead to the project at any given time. It provides a record that enables anyone to pick up work on it and have a full understanding of the history and aspirations in the event that the project leader is unable to.

The above requirements may seem onerous when applied, for example, to a job that is to be completed by one person in a couple of weeks, but the quality plan may be just a few notes in the front of the project file.

Standard cost plan pro forma

If a cost consultant has not been appointed you should identify project costs as far as you are able to, making sure you set out any caveats to the information provided. Refer to Fig 2.1 cost plan pro forma, which can be downloaded from www.ribabookshops.com/SPH. One way you can establish preliminary costs is through a preliminary tender process using the information you have to hand (drawings, outline specification, etc). Be clear with the contractors what you are doing but agree to include them on the actual tender list if they are prepared to help.

Fig 2.1

Cost plan pro forma

Job no: Job title:

Cost plan / budget estimate

		Cost of elements	Cost per m² gross floor area	Element shown as % of whole
Substructure				
Superstructure	Frame			
	Upper floors			
	Roof			
	Stairs			
	External cladding			
	Windows and external doors			
	Internal partitions			
	Internal doors and windows			
Internal finishes	Ceiling finishes			
	Wall finishes			
	Floor finishes			
Fittings	Furniture and fittings			
Services	Sanitary installation			
	Mechanical installation			
	Electrical installation			
	Special installations			
	Elevators and hoists			
	Builder's work			
	Builder's profit and attendance			
Building work	Sub-total			
Additional	Site works			
	Drainage			
	External services			
	Extra temporary works (phasing)			
	Inflation at 3%			
	Preliminaries at 5%			
Total	Excluding VAT and contingencies			

Architect:
And Architects

Date completed:
May 2014

Contract type:
JCT ICD 2011

This challenging site in Battersea, London, sits on an irregular plot created by the abutment of two perpendicular rows of Victorian terraced houses. The original building was set back within the site and was only 2.5m deep, providing very narrow rooms within the property. The client's main objective was to optimise the space available on the plot and design a modern four-storey family residence.

Through early discussions and pre-application meetings with the local authority (Wandsworth) it was apparent it would be feasible to increase the volume and footprint of the building. Site restrictions supported a case for a modern building design to make the best use of the space whilst making reference to the neighbouring buildings and not dominating the site. A modern design would also be the logical approach to take to support the Local Planning Policy Development Framework & NPPF.

In order to establish a brief, investigations were made into similar schemes that had been granted planning approval in the area; those of specific interest were approved projects, which filled a corner site at the junction of two roads. Following this, a review was carried out into the urban grain of the adjacent properties and surrounding street patterns.

The new proposal introduced large sections of glass which maximised natural light penetration into the property. The front corner windows have direct views down the street. The use of glazing on the ground floor and as a light shaft between the two elements of the property helped bring natural light into the heart of the living and dining areas which compensated for the lack of windows at the rear of the property.

A Concept Design Report was submitted as part of the planning application which included a Design and Access Statement: detailing the size, scale, appearance and layout of the new scheme, a Review of the Site Context showing similar schemes that had been granted approval in the area as well as modern buildings that have been approved in the Wandsworth Borough.

> Practice issues

Risk management

Risk management is a subject usually associated with large projects and large practices but it is a matter that should be addressed for all projects and practices, no matter what the size. Indeed, it could be argued that certain risks are more acute for the sole practitioner than they are for a larger business.

Risks should be assessed according to the likelihood of them occurring and the potential severity of their impact. A simple matrix can be developed to show these two variables and help determine the most significant issues. Having identified and assessed the risks, a strategy should be devised to mitigate them and communicated to relevant people throughout the practice.

Refer to:

— RIBA *Good Practice Guide: Keeping Out of Trouble*
— *Understanding Risk Management*, which can be downloaded from www.architectspi.com/Pages/RiskManagement.aspx

Included below are some of the key risks that a practice should factor into their plans:

RISK: Client goes into liquidation or does not pay fees owed, causing liquidity problems for the practice

— Agree a regular (ideally monthly) invoice and cash flow in your appointment.
— As far as possible make sure you are satisfied that your client is able to pay your fees.
— Ensure that you do not extend credit further than you can afford to lose. Assuming you have undertaken your work diligently, it is recommended that you do not continue if fees are outstanding more than 30 days later than the stipulated payment period (ie typically 60 days from the date of the invoice).
— Issue invoices promptly.

If you have carried out the work in accordance with the contract you should be paid for it on time. In such circumstances you must ensure you follow the provisions of your contract of appointment to the letter, including issuing any notices required. You are strongly advised not to take legal action unless as an absolute last resort. The outcome can be unpredictable, very time consuming and lead to a counter-claim, however unwarranted this may be.

RISK: Key member leaves at a critical time

— As far as possible consider what measures you would have to take should someone leave. Prevention is of course the best form of insurance, so try to keep your employees happy! Maintain regular dialogue with them about the 'soft' issues and perform personal reviews every 6–12 months.

RISK: Sub-letting work

— Practices may sometimes sub-let a part of their services – having first obtained the client's agreement. In these instances the architect should check that the person(s) or practice(s) they will subcontract the work to:
——— Have the necessary resources to perform the role.
——— Have the necessary skills and expertise to perform the role.
——— Have an appropriate level of PI insurance (and make annual checks that they maintain it for the 6 or 12 year liability period).
— A formal subcontract should be entered with the appropriate party on terms and conditions that are compatible with the architect's appointment with their client. It is particularly important to define fully and clearly the role that the sub-consultant is to perform, the deliverables that are their responsibility, and the timescale for performance of their part of the services.

RISK: Deteriorating workload leaves the practice with insufficient income

— Maintain a programme setting out your resourcing needs as far ahead as you are able to forecast and review it weekly. If you have to make difficult decisions about the size of your workforce you must do this as early as possible to mitigate the impact on the practice.

RISK: Disaster such as a fire or flooding occurring to the practice or its premises, rendering it difficult/impossible to fulfil its obligations

— Prepare a plan to deal with such matters such as cloud back-up systems and options for remote working.

RISK: Errors occurring on a project leading to a claim against the practice

Ensure that the right person is doing the task. Maintain a register of employee skills, qualifications, experience and in-house training.

> Stage summary

Stage 2 is where the creative design aspects of a project are focused and where architects can bring particular value through the development of efficient, effective and elegant design solutions that meet the client's brief. It also marks the conclusion of the briefing process.

In Stage 3, the conceptual design is developed into a fully coordinated one and usually submitted for planning approval.

Stage 3

Developed Design

RIBA Plan of Work 2013 Stage 3

RIBA
Plan of
Work
2013

Stage 3

Developed Design

Task Bar	Tasks
Core Objectives	Prepare **Developed Design**, including coordinated and updated proposals for structural design, building services systems, outline specifications, **Cost Information** and **Project Strategies** in accordance with **Design Programme**.
Procurement *Variable task bar*	*The Procurement activities during this stage will depend on the procurement route determined during Stage 1.*
Programme *Variable task bar*	*The RIBA Plan of Work 2013 enables this stage to overlap with a number of other stages depending on the selected procurement route.*
(Town) Planning *Variable task bar*	*It is recommended that planning applications are submitted at the end of this stage.*
Suggested Key Support Tasks	Review and update **Sustainability, Maintenance and Operational** and **Handover Strategies** and **Risk Assessments**. Undertake third party consultations as required and conclude **Research and Development** aspects. Review and update **Project Execution Plan**, including **Change Control Procedures**. Review and update **Construction** and **Health and Safety Strategies**. *During this stage it is essential to review the **Project Strategies** previously generated.*
Sustainability Checkpoints	• *Has a full formal sustainability assessment been carried out?* • *Have an interim Building Regulations Part L assessment and a design stage carbon/energy declaration been undertaken?* • *Has the design been reviewed to identify opportunities to reduce resource use and waste and the results recorded in the Site Waste Management Plan?*
Information Exchanges (at stage completion)	**Developed Design**, including the coordinated architectural, structural and building services design and updated **Cost Information**.
UK Government Information Exchanges	Required.

Introduction

Stage 3 maps broadly to the former Stage D but with greater emphasis on a fully coordinated design that is aligned to the Cost Information

The stage involves:

— Development of the Concept Design, typically in collaboration with other consultants such as structural and MEP services engineers and other specialist designers as appropriate.
— Typically at this stage the planning application will be submitted.

By the end of Stage 3 the architectural, building services and structural engineering designs will have been developed and coordinated, along with the Cost Information, and aligned to the Project Budget.

 Change Control Procedures should be established early in the project but at the latest by Stage 3. See Stage 2: Managing project-related change.

Project activities

Information required

1.	Stage 2 report.
2.	Final Project Brief.
3.	Stage 2 Concept Design, including design by other consultants and as accepted by the client in writing.
4.	Initial cost plan prepared by the cost consultant where appointed. Alternatively you might seek preliminary quotations from selected contractors and/or suppliers.
5.	Relevant technical data, regulations, planning policies, standards, etc.
6.	Project-specific information from potential subcontractors and suppliers.

Stage activities

1.	Review and update the Project Execution Plan, including the Change Control Procedures, Construction Strategy and Health and Safety Strategy.
2.	Confirm in writing with the client the proposed procurement method and the form of contract to be adopted.
3.	Advise the client on the need to appoint further consultants and specialists, which might include:

— Party wall surveyor.
— Daylight/sunlight/rights to light consultant.
— Code for Sustainable Homes/BREEAM assessor.
— Landscape architect.

If you know suitable companies be sure to recommend them. This can in itself be a good marketing or business development activity for future projects for your practice, and will help to engender collaborative working practices.

| 4. | Assess what input will be required from specialist firms, including potential subcontractors and suppliers. |

Discuss with the client and the design team:

— Whether any preliminary tender action for specialist subcontractors and suppliers will be required.
— Whether any action will be needed on advance orders (noting the risk involved in placing orders in advance of planning permission being granted).

| 5. | Confirm the programme and pattern for design team meetings. |

Note: for small projects it may not be necessary to hold formal design team meetings but if they are required, you must ensure that everyone in the team is aware of the Design Programme and when they need to provide information to others. You must also ensure the design outputs are properly reviewed and coordinated. The lead designer is responsible for facilitating the coordination of all information and its integration into the general scheme.

| 6. | Prepare the Developed Design, including coordinated and updated proposals for structural design, services systems, landscape, outline specifications, Cost Information and Project Strategies. |

| 7. | Draft preliminary specification notes. |

| 8. | Monitor, coordinate and integrate input from design team members and specialists. |

Maintain close collaboration with consultants and specialists. The architect might not be responsible for their individual performance, but will be responsible for the coordination and integration of their work into the overall design.

9.	Check the designers' cooperation with the principal designer with respect to the pre-construction information. As project lead or lead designer, the architect has an obligation (but not a legal duty) to check that every designer pays due regard to the CDM Regulations and avoids foreseeable risks, or takes steps to combat them at source when designing.

The principal designer must take all reasonable steps to ensure that designers comply with their duties.

Ensure that the Risk Register is kept up to date and developed alongside the design, not as a subsequent administration exercise. |
| 10. | Once the Stage 3 design has been approved by the client, prepare and submit the planning, listed building and conservation area applications as relevant.

Ensure that all applications are accompanied by relevant documents, including payment by the client of the appropriate fee. |
| 11. | Review and update the Sustainability Strategy (including interim Approved Document L assessment), the Maintenance and Operational Strategy and the Handover Strategy. |
| 12. | If instructed, issue party wall notices as soon as the proposals are sufficiently finalised, on behalf of the client. Consultations with users or third parties, and party wall matters, do not form part of the Services under the RIBA Standard Agreement 2010 (2012 revision), unless identified under Part 3 'Other Services', but note items 8 and 12 of the Agreement. |
| 13. | Provide the cost consultant with information for the cost plan and cash flow projection (or prepare a construction cost estimate if appointed to do so).

Discuss with the design team and the client the effect of major design decisions on the allocations within the cost plan before they are taken. There must be a regular two-way exchange of information if designers are to keep within cost targets or limits.

The cost consultant should collaborate with the architect and other consultants to develop and refine the full cost plan as the design is developed and outline specification notes are prepared. During this stage the cost consultant will prepare an elemental cost plan followed by a firm cost plan and cash flow forecast, relying on input from other design team members. |

They will then advise on the cost implications of compliance with statutory requirements.
The cost consultant should contribute information and advice for inclusion in the Stage 3
report to the client.

| 14. | If a BIM protocol is to be followed and you have been appointed as information manager: |

— Assist members of the design team to develop the design using the BIM model, ensuring that data-sharing protocols are followed.

— Check and sign off the BIM model at agreed stages.

— Issue or assist in the issue of design data at agreed times throughout the development of the design.

— Assist in the development of data relative to the agreed levels of detail.

— Assist in the integration of contractors', subcontractors' and suppliers' data into the BIM model.

| 15. | Prepare a Stage 3 report which should include: |

— The Developed Design.

— The planning submission drawings, reports and application forms.

— Cost plan.

— Target programme.

— Sustainability assessment.

If planning permission is refused

1. If planning permission is refused you will need to discuss the reasons why with the client and agree upon a way forward. There are a number of matters to bear in mind:

2. Make a note of the date of the planning decision/refusal, as appeal decisions are time-bound.

3. Note that the period for appeals is 12 weeks in some instances, or up to 6 months in others. Domestic projects generally have a shorter period.

4. All supporting information must be submitted with the application, not afterwards (this is a change to the previous procedure). You must therefore allow time for this when setting out a programme for appeal activities.

5. There are three options open:
   — appeal;
   — if you think the chances of a successful appeal are limited, make any amendments requested by the local authority and resubmit (you have one free go at this);
   — do both, ie resubmit and make a concurrent appeal. Note that the local authority might ask you to withdraw the appeal while they consider your proposal.

6. Ensure that the information submitted is the latest submitted version as the appeal will be invalidated if it is not.

7. For further information on the appeal process refer to www.planningportal.gov.uk/planning/appeals/guidance/guidanceontheappealprocess.

8. If there are technical reasons for the refusal the client may need to appoint specialists, eg daylight/sunlight consultant, etc.

9. It is worth noting that around one-third of appeals are allowed.

Information exchange

1.	The Developed Design, including the coordinated architectural, structural and mechanical services design. Drawings showing coordinated design, site layout, planning and spatial arrangements, elevational treatment, construction and environmental systems and buildability.
2.	Updated construction cost estimate.
3.	Where applicable, information for inclusion in pre-construction health and safety information to be passed to the principal designer.
4.	Proposals developed sufficiently to allow an application for full planning permission, listed building consent, conservation area consent, etc as applicable.
5.	Stage 3 report.

Sustainability Checkpoint 3

Sustainability aims

To ensure that the Developed Design reflects the Sustainability Strategy.

Key actions

1.	Review the Sustainability Strategy and ensure that the level of detail for any supporting strategies is developed, including those that impact on any statutory legislation.
2.	Produce a full formal sustainability assessment.
3.	Produce an interim Approved Document L assessment and design stage carbon/energy declaration (eg CarbonBuzz).
4.	Review the design to identify opportunities to reduce resource use and waste, and record this in the Site Waste Management Plan.
5.	Refine and distil the project's Sustainability Strategy, checking against brief and targets.
6.	Update energy modelling as the design develops, and check against targets.
7.	Refine the climate adaptation strategy and make provision for future adaptation interventions.
8.	Incorporate environmental and sustainability issues in the Planning Application Design and Access Statement, including a development of the Stage 2 'plain English' description of internal environmental conditions, seasonal control strategy and systems. Provide a supplementary detailed report if appropriate.

9.	Consider peer reviews of environmental control strategies and also involve stakeholders and users.
10.	Instigate initial involvement of contractors and specialist subcontractors where specialist products or systems are proposed; begin the process of obtaining their advice.
11.	Audit the Developed Design to ensure integration and compliance with the project's sustainability targets.

> Architect:
Barbara Weiss
Architects

Date completed:
August 2011

Construction cost:
£1m

Awards:
Nominated for Civic
Trust Award

The Wiener Library holds about 65,000 books, pamphlets, periodicals, memoirs, photographs, press cuttings and other materials, mainly on the subject of the Holocaust. With the lease of its previous premises about to expire, and after several years of searching, a substantial but dilapidated Grade II listed Georgian house in Russell Square was acquired for the purpose of providing a new home for the Library.

The architects sought to retain and respect the original Georgian fabric and details where existing, by restoring and reinstating elements such as the ornate cornices and architraves. New timber, stone and cork floors are sympathetic to the building's character and the occupiers' needs. Overall the project was sensitively and comprehensively designed to provide a sustainable home for the collection's future, while making the most of a limited budget that had to satisfy a variety of technical and programmatic demands.

Essential to the success of the project was the provision of a lift – both to allow the transfer of books and other materials from basement storage to first floor reading rooms, and to make the building fully accessible to disabled and elderly readers and staff. However, the provision of a lift in such a building was highly controversial, and was the subject of the first application. The assistance of both a planning consultant and a historic buildings consultant was obtained. The planning consultant coordinated the application process, took the lead in lobbying various consultees and neighbouring owners and produced the application documents. The historic buildings consultant advised on the development of a heritage strategy, and took responsibility for arguing the case in support of the architect's proposals.

Having obtained consent for the lift, the design of the project was developed in detail. A mezzanine in the reading room – a bold architectural statement that greatly increased the number of books directly available to readers – and internal details for decorative elements such as cornices and architraves were the subject of a second application.

Project issues

Strategies for planning success

It is good practice to:
— Confirm by letter or email all meetings, phone calls, etc with the planning authority.
— Make sure that the client or their representative attends all critical meetings with the planning authority.
— At an early stage consider project presentations to attract the interest and support of neighbourhood groups, etc.

Check the following:
— Dates and procedures of planning meetings.
— Probable date by which decision is to be given.
— Number and types of drawings required.
— Procedures, eg notices in the press, site notices.
— Processes for public consultation and response to any objections.

When making a planning application, check that:
— Forms are carefully completed – identify or list submitted drawings on forms or in a covering letter.
— An accurate site plan identifies the land concerned, clearly defined in red.
— A covering letter accompanies the application, explaining features of the scheme.
— An Ownership Certificate A (or B, C, D as appropriate) is served.
— Payment from the client for the appropriate sum is submitted at the same time (having checked the correct amount with the planning authority).
— The application is acknowledged by the planning authority, defining the start of the period for determination.
— A copy of the written report by the planning officer to the planning committee is obtained.
— If permitted and appropriate, oral representation is made to the planning committee.

If the application is made online through www.planningportal.gov.uk the system will automatically check you have provided the necessary documentation.

The planning meeting:

— Keep a written note of what is discussed at any meeting.
— If planning permission is refused and an appeal is contemplated, send your account of proceedings to the chief executive of the authority. If not contested, your account may have the status of 'agreed notes'. Examine the agenda and record of the meeting; these may constitute the basis for an appeal.

For more detailed advice on the planning process refer to *Town Planning: RIBA Plan of Work 2013 Guide.*

Design and Access Statement

A Design and Access Statement (DAS) is a short report accompanying and supporting a planning application which must be submitted:

— For a development which is a major development (both full and outline).
— Where any part of the development is in a designated area, with the development consisting of:
——— The provision of one or more dwelling houses.
——— The provision of a building or buildings where the floor space created by the development is 100m^2 or more.

A 'designated area' is:
— A conservation area.
— A property in a World Heritage Site.

The DAS is a means of explaining how a proposed development is a suitable response to the site and its setting, and of demonstrating that it can be adequately accessed by prospective users.

Lower thresholds apply in conservation areas and World Heritage Sites, where some smaller applications must also be accompanied by a DAS. Listed building consent applications must also include a DAS.

The DAS should set out:
— The design principles and concepts that have been applied to the development.
— How issues relating to access to the development have been dealt with.

A DAS must:
— Demonstrate the steps taken to appraise the context of the development and how the design of the development takes that context into account.
— Explain the design principles and concepts that have been applied to the development.
— Explain the applicant's approach to access and how relevant local planning policies have been taken into account, any consultation undertaken in relation to access issues, and how the outcome of this consultation has informed the proposed development.
— Explain how any specific issues that may affect access to the proposed development have been addressed.

The level of detail in a DAS should be proportionate to the complexity of the application. For straightforward planning applications, the DAS may only need to be a page long.

A DAS is not required for an application which is for a material change in use of the land or buildings.

BIM for small practices

Building Information Management (BIM) is increasingly important in the construction industry and although its impact is greater on larger projects, small projects can benefit from the implementation of BIM protocols and small practices can choose to establish themselves as being BIM-enabled, giving access to more complex projects and specialist workflows.

There are new roles open to anyone prepared to develop the skills, including information manager. The architect is arguably in the best position to act as information manager, responsible for developing, implementing and updating the BIM Execution Plan (see below); taking a lead in the planning, set-up and maintenance of the model, and leading the design team with regard to development of the design model and the protocols used.

There are a number of basic matters that need to be understood when undertaking BIM enabled projects:

BIM manual
The BIM manual, which should be located in the Project Execution Plan, sets out file and drawing naming conventions and other processes in relation to BIM on a design team basis. Agreement of the BIM manual is a core requirement in the development of a collaborative project team.

BIM execution plan
The BEP, which should be included in the Project Execution Plan and is part of the Technology Strategy, should set out: the parameters of the project; project team members; the BIM standards to be used; the deliverables from the model; the software to be used; the data exchange method; the file naming convention; a schedule of quality control checks; and a schedule of dates for review of the model by the design team.

A pro forma BIM execution plan can be found at www.ribabookshops.com/SPH.

Level of detail (LOD)
Although CAD information is produced 'full size', consideration must be given to the stage the project is at and the purpose for which it will be used. For each project/model, a spreadsheet should be prepared setting out, by building element, the level of detail at each stage (0 to 7), alongside the author of that design. Members of the design team should consult the information manager for advice on BIM protocols and procedures.

The standard definitions for a LOD system are outlined below, although some clients may operate their own definition system. A LOD agreement form should be completed and agreed by the relevant parties. A pro forma agreement can be found at www.ribabookshops.com/SPH.

Level of Detail (LOD)

LOD 100:
Overall building massing indicative of area, height, volume, location and orientation.

Potential deliverables/output:
Area analysis studies based on net/gross areas, basic environmental analysis, basic construction cost estimates based on floor areas.

LOD 200:
Information modelled as generalised systems or assemblies with approximate quantities, size, shape, location and orientation. Other non-geometric information may be attached to the model elements.

Potential deliverables/output:
Basic output of GA plans, elevations, GA sections etc, improvement of accuracy of construction cost estimates from LOD 100, increased cost certainty, basic door/window schedules – quantities and approximate sizes, more detailed environmental analysis from LOD 100, initial estimates of material quantities, increased accuracy of area analysis.

LOD 300:
Information modelled as specific assemblies, accurate in terms of quantity, size, shape, location and orientation. Other non-geometric information may be attached to the model elements.

LOD 400:

Information modelled as specific assemblies that are accurate in terms of quantity, size, shape, location and orientation with complete fabrication, assembly and detailing information. Other non-geometric information may be attached to the model elements.

LOD 500:

Model elements modelled as constructed assemblies, accurate in terms of quantity, size, shape, location and orientation. Other non-geometric information may be attached to the model elements.

The level of detail expected at each stage might be as follows:

Stages 0–1	LOD 100
Stage 2	LOD 100–200
Stage 3	LOD 200–300
Stage 4	LOD 300–400
Stage 5	LOD 400–500

For further information go to www.bimtaskgroup.org.

Architect:
Stephen Turvil Architects

Date completed:
June 2012

Construction cost:
£210,000

Awards:
Shortlisted – AJ Small
Projects Award 2013

This project involved the demolition of an existing redundant telephone exchange, the change of use of the site to residential, and the construction of a two-storey, two-bedroom dwelling.

The site lies within the limits of development for the village and within the Great Bedwyn Conservation Area and an Area of Outstanding Natural Beauty. The site has a rural feel and is located along the southwestern edge of the village, bordering a large plot of allotments along its western boundary.

The layout and positioning of the house was largely determined by the hedge that runs along the northern boundary and by the positioning of the existing old exchange building. It was important that such a significant hedge was not destroyed, as it is an important part of the visual amenity of the area and provides a screen to the lower floor of the building.

Rather than develop a property that had an appearance based on a pastiche of the existing village houses we decided on a strategy that responded to the more rural context; an architecture that takes inspiration from the local farm buildings and from the sheds and shelters of the adjacent allotment.

The new house is conceived as a simple elemental structure with a purposeful aesthetic reminiscent of the local vernacular barns. It is a rectangular structure with a steep pitched roof and gable ends. The external finishes take inspiration from the rural vernacular, with black stained larch horizontal cladding being the predominant material. Black buildings work well visually within a green backdrop.

Practice issues

IT management

The RIBA *Handbook of Practice Management, 9th edition* contains a chapter on IT management and gives guidance on use of the internet, BIM, setting up an IT system and general good practice for CAD and IT systems. The following are some key issues for consideration in relation to running a small practice. Refer also to Stage 3: BIM for small practices.

Backing up

Backing up data is important for obvious reasons, but many practices either neglect to or do it with insufficient regularity. Once a week should be considered the absolute minimum, but daily is appropriate and you should consider what quantity of information you could really afford to lose if something did go wrong.

Cloud-based systems will effectively give you continuous back-up but can be expensive and slow. As an alternative you can just store essential data online (accounts, payroll, quality systems, etc). For further advice go to www.cloudwards.net/online-backup-vs-external-hard-drive.

For larger files (eg CAD, BIM and images) use a portable hard drive coupled with back-up software – a 1TB drive is relatively cheap, meaning two can be purchased to ensure back-ups alternate and can be stored off site.

If you want to use a cloud service to store and transport files then the free services of Dropbox, Google Drive and Microsoft Box can provide a fair amount of online storage which can be increased if you opt for the paid-for service. www.wuala.com is a paid-for, encrypted storage facility that can be used for backing up important and confidential documents. Alternatively for project-related information you could use Woobius (www.woobius.com) which is a CDE (common desktop environment) pay-as-you-use facility.

For further advice on online back-up go to:

www.techradar.com/news/internet/cloud-services/best-cloud-backup-10-online-backup-services-tested-1176843

www.techradar.com/news/internet/best-cloud-storage-dropbox-vs-skydrive-vs-google-drive-vs-icloud-1120024

Software and information management

Small practices may benefit from sharing software licences between individuals (as opposed to having network versions). Software is generally licensed per number of users, but if different people are working on different applications at different stages of a project they will require one only when actually using the software. If there is a small server-controlled network, then installing the licence and applications to the server and allocating the rights to the software as it is opened on a terminal means that the number required will be less than 100% of the workstations.

Following this method means that users must make sure they close an application once they have completed a piece of work. Licences can be assigned per user or per application, or alternatively, developers can offer some form of annual membership or licence that enables each upgrade of the software that year to be received free of charge, based on a fee per user over and above the licence costs (which may be discounted in this instance).

It is important to ensure that software will be compatible before deciding on a mainstream application. Interoperability will avoid the more time-consuming and costly process of redrawing the design, and the potential loss of data each time impacts are assessed in different applications, as opposed to simply transferring a design from one to the other.

Mainstream 2D and 3D packages may also offer 'light' versions with reduced functionality, which may suit both budget and aspirations, but it is worth researching what the likely upgrade costs and what the potential development of the software will be in the future. Furthermore, given the significant development and investment towards the production of a single project model, utilising intelligent components, it is important to understand whether the software chosen, if not a BIM application, can be upgraded to offer a BIM solution.

Although special hardware is not required for 2D drafting and some 3D modelling (except perhaps a high-quality graphics card), if BIM is ultimately the preferred route then the software may be much more memory intensive and require faster, larger processors and graphics cards, which in turn will impact on the workstations used. In addition to CAD packages it is likely that the practice will be investing in desktop publishing software, database and scheduling software, programming and graphic/image manipulation, financial management and project management applications and many others. As with hardware, it is important to take into account compatibility, durability, flexibility and adaptability to the business and the future of the business, when assessing which software package is the most appropriate.

> ## Stage summary

Moving from Stage 3 to Stage 4 marks the transition from the iterative design stages to the linear ones. Stage 4 design should develop within the clear physical and financial parameters established at the end of Stage 3 and should therefore be predictable – a matter of filling in the gaps. There are of course important design decisions to be made with regard to specification and detail – the latter often being more open to scrutiny on small projects than large ones.

Stage 3 usually ends with a planning decision but in the Plan of work 2013 the design is fully coordinated and integrated with the cost plan.

Section III

Preparing to Build

Introduction

Stage 4: Technical Design and Procurement (of the contractor) have been grouped together in this section as activities lying between the iterative design stages and the construction stage.

Technical Design activities should be entirely linear and predictable, adding detail within the agreed spatial zoning and pricing structure of the coordinated Stage 3 Developed Design. That is not to say that it is not a creative stage, as clearly there are important matters to be determined about the quality and appearance of the building, but that the parameters should be pre-determined by the end of Stage 3.

Stage 4 is where the architectural and engineering designs are fully developed, along with input from any specialist subcontractors or suppliers. Where the architect is the lead designer, he/she will have a responsibility to review this information and ensure that it is integrated into the coordinated design. Stage 4 activities can overlap with Stage 5, depending on the form of procurement. Under traditional procurement where tendering occurs after completion of the Technical Design there may be technical queries raised by the contractor and these are a Stage 5 activity.

Procurement is a flexible task bar under the Plan of Work 2013 but for small projects will typically occur after Stage 4, when sufficient information has been prepared. This will minimise the risk of variations due to missing information and reduced quality due to unresolved specification information.

The form of Procurement and the information provided for tendering can have a significant impact on the quality and cost of a project and it is important therefore to ensure that the documentation provided to tenderers is complete and coordinated.

 It is critical to allow sufficient resources (ie fee) to develop all the information to an appropriate level of detail, to ensure the constructor has sufficient data to construct the building. The single largest factor in claims and subsequent legal costs is insufficient, uncoordinated or inaccurate production information.

Stage 4

Technical Design

RIBA Plan of Work 2013 Stage 4

RIBA
Plan of
Work
2013

Stage 4

Technical Design

Task Bar	Tasks
Core Objectives	Prepare **Technical Design** in accordance with **Design Responsibility Matrix** and **Project Strategies** to include all architectural, structural and building services information, specialist subcontractor design and specifications, in accordance with **Design Programme**.
Procurement Variable task bar	*The Procurement activities during this stage will depend on the procurement route determined during Stage 1.*
Programme Variable task bar	*The RIBA Plan of Work 2013 enables this stage to overlap with a number of other stages depending on the selected procurement route.*
(Town) Planning Variable task bar	*The RIBA Plan of Work 2013 suggests that any conditions attached to a planning consent are addressed during this stage, prior to work starting on site during Stage 5.*
Suggested Key Support Tasks	Review and update **Sustainability, Maintenance and Operational** and **Handover Strategies** and **Risk Assessments**. Prepare and submit Building Regulations submission and any other third party submissions requiring consent. Review and update **Project Execution Plan**. Review **Construction Strategy**, including sequencing, and update **Health and Safety Strategy**. *A further review of the **Project Strategies** and documentation previously generated is required during this stage.*
Sustainability Checkpoints	• *Is the formal sustainability assessment substantially complete?* • *Have details been audited for airtightness and continuity of insulation?* • *Has the Building Regulations Part L submission been made and the design stage carbon/energy declaration been updated and the future climate impact assessment prepared?* • *Has a non-technical user guide been drafted and have the format and content of the Part L log book been agreed?* • *Has all outstanding design stage sustainability assessment information been submitted?* • *Are building **Handover Strategy** and monitoring technologies specified?* • *Have the implications of changes to the specification or design been reviewed against agreed sustainability criteria?* • *Has compliance of agreed sustainability criteria for contributions by specialist subcontractors been demonstrated?*
Information Exchanges (at stage completion)	Completed **Technical Design** of the project.
UK Government Information Exchanges	Not required.

Introduction

Stage 4 maps broadly to the former Stage F and is the point at which the iterative design process has completed and the Technical Design (or production information) is developed, which should be an entirely 'linear' (and therefore lean) process.

The stage involves:

— Preparing the Technical Design (production information) for use in the tender documents (for traditional procurement) and to inform construction activities on site. Work should be allocated between design team members and specialist suppliers and subcontractors in accordance with the Design Responsibility Matrix and Project Strategies.
— Under traditional procurement, preliminary considerations regarding the tender list or initial discussions with a preferred contractor should also take place at this stage in readiness for the tender process. If the contractor or specialists have already been engaged, the designers will be able to work collaboratively with them to improve efficiency and value.

The skill set required for Technical Design is of course somewhat different to that required for the previous, Concept and Developed Design, stages. Some find this stage rewarding and enjoy the rigour required; others prefer the more contemplative, open design activities of the initial stages of the process. Some bring different skills altogether such as business development, legal aptitude or office management but all are required for a rounded practice. In a micro practice one person may need to have a range of skills, but it is increasingly difficult to practise as a generalist, and micro-scale practitioners (and others) should consider forming collaborations to broaden their offering.

Project activities

Information required

1.	Stage 3 report.
2.	Planning application information including the Developed Design, the planning approval notice and planning conditions.
3.	Construction cost estimate from Stage 3.
4.	Relevant technical data and samples from potential suppliers.

Stage activities

1.	Establish the scope of the activities to be carried out during this stage and produce a Design Programme that meets the overall Project Programme. Check that available staff resources are both sufficient and appropriate. Progress should be monitored regularly (say once a week) and if found to be slipping, the necessary actions should be taken to bring the work back on track.

Development of production information should be a 'linear' process and therefore easily programmable. You should have a change control process in place. See Stage 2: Managing project-related change.

Make sure the client is aware of this and that any changes to the approved Developed Design which are client-originated might mean abortive work, additional fees and expenses and delays.

2.	Obtain the client's approval of materials and finishes. Obtain samples and submit to the client for approval.
3.	Discuss with the client whether interviews with potential contractors should take place at this stage. Under certain circumstances contractors' views on operational methods and health and safety during construction could be valuable.

4.	Review the implications of any conditions attached to the planning permission with the design team and discuss these with the planning officer as necessary.
5.	Prepare the Technical Design and coordinate it with design output developed by other consultants and sub-contractors. See 'Information Exchange' below for a list of information that might be required.
6.	As the Technical Design develops, review and update the Sustainability, Maintenance and Operation and Handover strategies. Review the Construction Strategy, including sequencing and programme, and update the Health and Safety Strategy. Review and update the Project Execution Plan.
7.	Continue discussions with the Building control and fire authorities and prepare a building notice for submission under the Building Regulations, or an application for approval by deposit of full plans. *See Stage 4: Building Control applications.*
8.	Continue discussions with relevant authorities for highways, drainage, water, gas, electricity supplies, etc. *The local authority's website will usually have contact details of the various bodies.*
9.	If they have not yet been served (in Stage 3) and if instructed, issue party wall and/ or foundation notices on behalf of the client. If notices are being issued by others, check that all notices have been served. See Stage 4: Party wall procedures.
10.	On BIM-enabled projects, if you have been appointed as information manager: — Assist members of the design team to develop the design using the BIM model, ensuring that data-sharing protocols are followed. — Check and sign off the model at agreed stages.

— Issue or assist in the issue of design data at agreed times throughout the development of the design.
— Assist in the development of data relative to the agreed levels of detail.
— Assist in the integration of contractor's, subcontractors' and suppliers' data into the BIM model.

| 11. | On BIM-enabled projects: |

— Carry out detailed modelling, integration and analysis using the BIM model.
— Create Technical Design level parametric objects for all major elements (where appropriate information exists this may be based on Tier 2 suppliers' information).
— Integrate subcontractor performance-specified work information into the BIM model data.
— Undertake a final review and sign-off of the BIM model.
— Enable contractor access to the BIM.
— Review construction sequencing (4D) with the contractor.
— Share data for conclusion of design coordination and detailed analysis with subcontractors.

| 12. | Provide information for the cost consultant to prepare a pre-tender construction cost estimate (or prepare a pre-tender construction cost estimate if appointed to do so) where using traditional procurement. |

The pre-tender construction cost estimates is an essential check prior to inviting tenders. At this point the estimate should be an accurate prediction of the tender figures. The design and tender documents may need to be amended if the estimate does not match the project brief.

Review with the client the implications of the pre-tender estimate.

Discuss possible options with the client. Explain implications for timetable and consultants' fees if amendments are required to change (or comply with) the brief.

| 13. | Amend the Technical Design if necessary following cost checks. |

14.	If the programme for tendering needs to be maintained, establish whether changes are to be reflected in the Building Contract documents (which will then differ from the tender documents) or whether amendments are to be the subject of immediate variations under instruction by the contract administrator when the Building Contract has been entered into.
15.	Check the effects of any amendments on specialist subcontract work and arrange for adjusted tenders if necessary.
16	Prepare the Stage 4 report, which should include:

— Final cost plan.

— Estimated construction contract programme.

— Copies of all Technical Design information.

— A note of any planning conditions.

— Building Regulations approval (if undertaken through the 'Full Plans' route).

Information exchange

1.	Technical Design coordinated documents - probably including location, component and assembly drawings, schedules, specifications and schedules of work. .
2.	Specification notes (prescriptive and performance) on materials and workmanship, systems, products, execution, etc.
3.	Information for preparation of full plans submission for approval under the Building Regulations.
4.	Non-technical information for use in dealings with third parties, landlords, tenants, funders, etc (eg in connection with leases, boundaries, party walls).
5.	Information for inclusion in pre-construction health and safety information to be passed to the principal designer.

It is good practice to drip-feed this to the principal designer throughout the design phase as it becomes available.

6.	Updated construction cost estimate.

7.	Stage 4 report.

Sustainability Checkpoint 4

Sustainability aims

Ensure that the final design prepared by both design team and any specialist subcontractors reflects the requirements of the Sustainability Strategy.

Key actions

1.	Check that the formal sustainability assessment is substantially complete.
2.	Check that details have been audited for airtightness and continuity of insulation.
3.	Check that the implications of changes to the specification or design has been reviewed against agreed sustainability criteria.
4.	Make Approved Document L submission, design stage carbon/energy declaration update and future climate impact assessment.
5.	Draft the non-technical user guide and agree the format and content of the Approved Document L log book.
6.	Submit all outstanding design stage sustainability assessment information.
7.	Assess the compliance of contributions by specialist consultants and contractors with agreed sustainability criteria demonstrated.
8.	Specify the building handover process and monitoring technologies.
9.	Agree technical requirements to support the monitoring strategy.
10.	Ensure that artificial lighting and daylighting strategies and controls are mutually supportive in delivering low-energy consumption.

11.	Involve building users in reviewing the environmental control systems and manual and automatic controls to ensure that they are appropriately simple and intuitive, and that there is a match between expectations and the design.
12.	Make sure that the project team is aware of the technical consequences of strategic sustainability decisions.
13.	Specify sustainable materials and products, balancing life-cycle assessment, maintenance regime, durability and cost.
14.	Complete consultation with subcontractors and suppliers with regard to Technical Design issues and review information packages to check that they are coordinated, complementary and support all components of the Sustainability Strategy.
15.	Agree responsibilities and routines for data recording to monitor performance.
16.	Review the potential knock-on implications of any value engineering on performance and sustainability targets.
17.	Review the final details, including subcontractors' packages, for airtightness and continuity of insulation.
18.	Review the information required to demonstrate compliance with sustainability requirements (eg materials certification).

> **Architect:**
> Chris Dyson
> Architects

Date completed:
October 2013

Construction cost:
£130,000

Awards:
Finalist - AJ Retrofit
Awards (2014)

Originally a warehouse, this building was being used as a house but suffered from a lack of natural light and ventilation to the ground floor bedroom. An existing shed to the rear of the bedroom and a small, unventilated ensuite bathroom compromised the ability to bring light and air into this space. On the first floor an unappealing painted GRP roof comprised the external roof terrace space accessed via a small side door from a closet wing containing a kitchen.

We were appointed by a private client to resolve the light ingress and ventilation problems on the ground floor along with providing enhanced ensuite bathroom accommodation. On the ground floor the brief was to create an enhanced roof terrace space with external lighting and better connection from terrace to living spaces that didn't rely on access from the kitchen. The upper floor required minor cosmetic refurbishment.

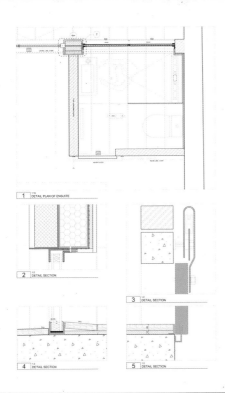

1 | DETAIL PLAN OF ENSUITE

2 | DETAIL SECTION

3 | DETAIL SECTION

4 | DETAIL SECTION

5 | DETAIL SECTION

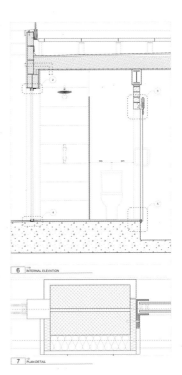

6 | INTERNAL ELEVATION

7 | PLAN DETAIL

The architects resolved the problems on the ground floor by removing the shed structure at the rear of the property and opening up a small courtyard with new glass doors on to the bedroom. The ensuite was also reconfigured with an entire wall of glass to the private courtyard bringing in air and natural light. A large walk-on rooflight was added to the terrace above which floods the bedroom with natural light, controllable via an electronic blind system.

On the ground floor, a small window from the living spaces to the roof terrace was replaced with a large-format steel-framed glazed door. An inclined area to the bedroom below was replaced with translucent glass with powder-coated metal mesh steps to allow access to the new roof terrace. The mesh is removable to allow the inclined rooflights to be cleaned. The original GRP roof was removed, insulated and replaced with a new GRP roof finished with natural stone panels on adjustable feet. A perimeter privacy screen of Iroko wood with discreet downlighting and a glass balustrade to the lower courtyard completes the external refurbishment.

Project issues

Collaborative team work

To optimise the design process it is important to establish collaborative workflow. Industry-standard advice on this can be found in PAS1192, which is freely available at http://shop.bsigroup.com/forms/PASs/PAS-1192-2 and http://shop.bsigroup.com/forms/PASs/PAS-1192-3/.

You should also refer to the BIM Task Group website:

www.bimtaskgroup.org/pas-1192-22013.

Note: PAS1192 is generally aimed at larger projects and some of the protocols may be considered too onerous for small projects but you should be aware of them and implement the advice as appropriate in each case.

Especially during Stage 4 you should check that any design changes are recorded and subject to the Change Control Procedures. No design team members should attempt to make decisions unilaterally.

The lead designer should facilitate the coordination and integration of information from design team members.

Technical Design advice

In developing the Technical Design consider the following:

— Prepare the Technical Design in accordance with the Design Responsibility Matrix and Project Strategies.
— Include all architectural, structural and mechanical services information and specifications.
— Ensure that the lead designer reviews and signs off all information.
— Drawings:
—— Prepare a schedule of drawings and other information needed.
—— Draw up a programme for the preparation and delivery of the drawings and the other stage outputs and assess the resource required to complete it in line with the programme.
—— Confirm a system for recording and distributing information and revisions.
—— Use standard title panels for all drawings and try to limit the number of different sizes of drawings; A1 and A3 are generally the preferred sizes for hard-copy drawing output.
—— Compile specification notes as relevant during the production of drawn information.
— Specifications and schedules:
—— Agree a strategy and programme for the production of appropriate documents with the design team.
—— Assemble specification notes made during Stage 3.
—— Prepare a checklist to show which headings or subheadings might be relevant for the particular project.
—— Allocate responsibilities for writing particular parts of the specification.
—— Select specification sections and clauses from a standard specification library (NBS Create is recommended).
—— Establish which parts will be by prescription and which by performance requirements.
—— Review the selection of materials, descriptions of workmanship, etc and check with the cost plan.
—— Check the final copy for errors, omissions and possible inconsistencies, either within parts of the document or between the specification and other Technical Design information.
— To assist the cost consultant during preparation of the information for tendering, the architect might be expected to supply the following:
—— Specification or specification notes for incorporation in work sections.
—— Information for inclusion in preliminaries such as:

-------- Form of contract, supplements, option clauses, amended clauses, etc.
-------- Content and use of contract documentation.
-------- Method statements required.
-------- Pre-tender health and safety information.
-------- Work to be done by the employer direct.
-------- Requirements concerning sequence, time limitations, etc.
-------- Provisional sums to be included.
-------- Provision for named subcontractors/suppliers.
-------- Any explanatory diagrams that are required.
-------- Overall dimensions and internal dimensions of all rooms and spaces.

 For advice on the scope, format and content of production information refer to the Construction Project Information Committee (CPIC) website www.cpic.org.uk which contains advice and a number of useful, industry-standard publications.

Specifications

The specification is of course a critical tool in delivering the appropriate level of quality and ensuring proper building performance. Many established practices have a standard format for specification and project preliminaries, but for those starting afresh it is important to head off in the right direction. And for those using standard formats it is essential that the clauses are reviewed for each project to ensure they meet current regulations and standards.

 The specification process should start from the earliest design stages, with notes kept on file in preparation for assembling the final, full version. This is important from a project cost management point of view and will help the cost consultant to make a meaningful assessment at each stage.

NBS is the industry standard, and general advice on best practice and information on their products can be found at www.thenbs.com.

NBS Create will guide you through the specification process and can be used from the outset, starting with an initial outline specification which can be developed into a performance and then fully detailed specification. It also contains project management sections that deal with non-technical items such as description of the site, project participants and the contract. Contents are arranged using the Uniclass classification system, including linked contract, outline, performance, product, execution and completion clauses. All of the clauses contain drop-down values linked to guidance and product information. It is regularly and automatically updated online, providing technically robust pre-written system, performance, product, execution and completion clauses.

Refer also to the *RIBA Job Book, 9th edition* Stage 4.

Building Control applications

Building Control submissions can be dealt with either as a 'full plans' submission or using the 'building notice' procedure.

Full plans
Under this method, drawings, calculations and so on are submitted for approval prior to work on site commencing. This is usual for anything more than a small house extension. There is a statutory timescale for the response from a local authority inspector.

Building notice
Under this method, work can commence 48 hours after submission of the notice and the work is monitored by the inspector as it progresses. You must be certain that the works will comply, otherwise there is a risk that non-compliant work will have to be taken down and rebuilt in accordance with the regulations. It can only be used for extensions to dwelling houses and not for new builds, or other building uses.

Approved inspectors
Compliance can be certified either by the local authority or by an approved inspector. A list of approved inspectors can be obtained from the Construction Industry Council: www.cic.org.uk. Approved inspectors use an 'initial notice' procedure which takes the place of a 'full plans' application. You will need to agree upon what information is provided to the approved inspector, who will advise you on what is required.

Site inspection
Whichever method is followed, site inspection will be a part of the process and notice must be given before works such as foundations, drainage, steelwork erection and construction of walls or floors commence. Notification should also be given upon completion, prior to occupation.

Scotland
The method in Scotland is similar but is undertaken through a 'Building Warrant'.

Further advice

Further advice including free downloadable copies of all the Approved Documents, an explanation of the approval process, the Code for Sustainable Homes and various good-practice guides can all be found at www.planningportal.gov.uk/buildingregulations.

Note that at the time of going to press the government has announced plans to integrate the Code for Sustainable Homes into the Building Regulations in 2015.

Party wall procedures

The government has published 'Party Wall etc Act 1996: Explanatory booklet' (June 2013) to provide straightforward explanations of the conditions requiring party wall or foundation notices and sample letters for issuing to adjoining owners and responses that can be sent to them to reply with.

There are three different forms of notice that relate to:

— Work on an existing party wall.
— Building up against or astride the boundary line.
— Excavation near neighbouring buildings (ie for foundations).

If a party wall surveyor is to be appointed he/she will manage this process but will need copies of the relevant architectural and structural drawings to submit.

If the adjoining owners have agreed that no surveyor will be required they can exchange letters, using the standard forms in the guidebook.

The guidebook with the standard letters can be downloaded for free. Search for 'party wall booklet' on www.planningportal.gov.uk.

Cost planning

An essential part of good design is managing cost, both of your own resources (people, materials, services, etc) and of the project. You should discuss the Project Budget with the client at the outset and monitor estimated construction cost at regular intervals and at least at every design stage (1/2/3/4).

If a cost consultant is not appointed you can either make an assessment by benchmarking similar, recent projects or approach a contractor to give you advice. In exchange you can agree to include them on the tender list.

If neither of these options is available you must make sure the client is aware that the design proposals may need to be amended to take account of tender prices that exceed the budget, and that this is likely to attract additional design consultancy cost and could delay the project.

Assuming you have cost advice during the design stages:

— Discuss with the design team and the client the effect of detailed design decisions on the allocations within the cost plan before implementation.
— Provide information to the cost consultant for revision of the construction cost estimate and cash flow projection (or revise the construction cost estimate if appointed to do so).
— Report to the client on cost matters at agreed intervals.
— Review quotations received from specialist firms and check against provisional sums or budget figures.
— Adopt a formal approach to 'question and answer' procedures with the cost consultant at an early stage.
— Establish a cut-off point for information to be passed to the cost consultant prior to tendering. Any subsequent changes will then need to be treated as contract variations at the appropriate time.

> **Architect:**
> West Architecture

Date completed:
February 2013

Construction cost:
£350,000

Awards:
Commendation –
New London Awards
2014 (retail category)

Photography:
Ben Blossom

The Well & Bucket pub forms the centrepiece of a Grade II listed terrace, the restoration of which was undertaken by Julian Harrap Architects. The terrace is at the north end of Brick Lane, within the Redchurch Street Conservation Area. This is an area that is currently in a state of flux as the energy of Shoreditch moves slowly east.

The building had been used as a leather wholesaler since the mid-1980s. After initially obtaining planning permission for change of use, a number of separate listed building consents were required during the course of the project, as opening up revealed a variety of unexpected features and elements.

This project is much more about discovery, preservation and soft interventions rather than making architectural statements with new elements. It is also exemplary of our role for ongoing client, Barworks, where we act as executive architect in their development of restaurants and bars in central London. For them, most of what we do is invisible, providing technical back-up for the delivery of their projects whilst obtaining statutory approvals and advising on sites from the outset.

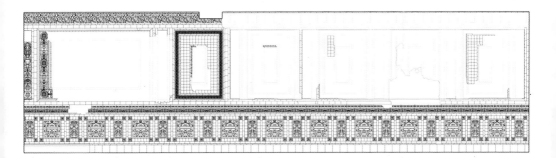

Upon the acquisition of this site, we were presented with a plasterboard-lined box with no visible suggestion of what lay beyond the lining. We had previously researched the building and knew that in the past there were a number of Victorian tiled murals by William B Simpson. Established in 1833, the company is now trading as WB Simpson & Sons and has more recently been associated with the Olympic Aquatics Centre and Ironmonger Row Baths.

Although we knew of the tiles' presence, we did not know their condition. It transpired that the majority of the tiles had been removed in the 1980s, the remnants of which were revealed after being hidden behind plasterboard for 30 years. Removal of the existing suspended ceiling revealed a hidden rooflight which has also been restored. Panelled wall linings and a new ceiling conceal an engineered acoustic construction which separates the bar from adjacent residential units to one side and above.

Practice issues

Managing the office team

The RIBA *Handbook of Practice Management, 9th edition* (2013) contains a chapter on people management, which offers comprehensive information on the legal as well as the 'soft' issues of management, but the following are some other key issues to be considered.

If your workload is of a size that means you are unable to undertake it all yourself there are a number of ways of engaging with others to assist you:

— Collaboration with another practitioner or practice through sub-consultancy.
— Temporary engagement of individual(s) for a specific piece of work.
— Employing full-time staff.

Regardless of how you engage them, people are the most important asset of any practice. Keeping them motivated is important to maintain the quality of work produced. Communication is crucial, and keeping staff well-briefed and informed of projects and practice aims, ambitions and developments is key to keeping them motivated and productive, whatever the size of the business.

The RIBA Code of Professional Conduct (available from www.architecture.com) places various requirements on members in relation to employment of staff. The *RIBA Chartered Practice Manual* also sets out various criteria to be met by chartered practices, including the establishment and following of a model RIBA Employment Policy that sets out the roles and rights of the RIBA, the Chartered Practice and the employee (for details, go to www. architecture.com and search for 'employment policy') The RIBA publishes a model employment contract for students undertaking practical training. Note also the requirement for RIBA Chartered Practices on remuneration of students.

There are a number of useful guidance notes/updates on employment law, including:

— The RIBA Employment Policy (see above).
— Workplace Law Network (www.workplacelaw.net).
— The employment section of the DirectGov website (www.direct.gov.uk/en/Employment).
— Labour Relations Agency (www.lra.org.uk/index/employment_legislation).

The RIBA operates an HR and Employment Law service for RIBA Chartered Practices in the 'members only' area of its website (www.architecture.com) which covers a comprehensive range of topics, offers a 'help page' and includes telephone contact details for other queries.

There are strict regulations governing the employment of non-UK or EU nationals, and in most cases a work permit will be required. Non-UK and European nationals may not be employed legally unless their right to work in the UK can be verified, and practices are strongly advised to check this right for all employees, and retain evidence confirming this.

 Guidance for employers is provided by the Home Office on the UK Border Agency website (www.ukba.homeoffice.gov.uk/employers).

In general, other than for certain specialised types of employment, the potential employee will require a sponsor (which will usually be the practice), and the process of applying for the necessary permit should be started as early as possible.

> ## Stage summary

The Technical Design stage is perhaps the most critical in terms of risk management. Research shows that most construction litigation arises from poor or missing Technical Design information, so it is essential that enough time and resources (ie fees) are allocated to do the job properly. If you do not feel comfortable with producing the information to a sufficient standard, seek advice from peers or more experienced practitioners, either within your practice or outside it.

Under the RIBA Plan of Work 2013, Procurement (of the contractor) can take place anywhere from the end of Stage 1 onwards. For most small projects however it will occur either after the development of the Technical Design or, as can be the case with domestic extensions, after Stage 3 when planning permission has been obtained, and using the planning application drawings. This is not recommended for situations where the client wants to maintain control of quality. Where an architect has been appointed it is usual for tendering to take place with a full set of Technical Design information.

Procurement

Introduction

The Procurement stage is when tendering or other methods of contractor engagement are undertaken. Procurement is a variable task bar in the Plan of Work 2013 reflecting the fact that it occurs at different times depending on the method of Procurement adopted for the project. The activities map to those in the former Stages G and H.

Whilst Procurement is a flexible task bar in the Plan of Work 2013 rather than a work stage, it has been given a separate section in this book to explain the important activities that take place when appointing the contractor.

The stage involves:

— Collating all the Technical Design information.
— Preparing tender documentation.
— Either:
——— Seeking competitive tenders or
——— Negotiating a price with one contractor.
— Assessing the tender proposal and making a recommendation to the Employer (client).
— Notifying unsuccessful tenderers and giving them Feedback.

Tendering is generally managed by either the architect, the cost consultant or the project manager if one has been appointed.

With small projects it is usual for it to take place once all the Technical Design information has been completed but this will not always be the case. Refer to 'Procurement: Construction contracts' below.

Project activities

Information required

1. Information for tendering:

— Technical Design information.
— Pre-construction health and safety information.
— Completed tender documents from any named subcontractors and suppliers, with all sections properly completed.
— Completed particulars for the Building Contract and any supplements for the form of contract selected.
— Any conditions imposed by the local building control and fire authorities, particularly relating to construction details and fire prevention, including finishes.

Stage activities

Note: these activities can take place simultaneously with Stage 4 or potentially Stage 3, or be carried out once Stage 4 work has been completed. The decision will depend on the relative importance of time, cost and quality.

1. Collate the final Technical Design information and prepare, coordinate, collate and check the tender documents. These should include:

— Technical Design information.
— Form of contract with completed particulars.
— Pre-construction health and safety information.
— Completed tender documents from any named subcontractors and suppliers, with all sections properly completed.
— Any conditions imposed by the local building control and fire authorities, particularly relating to construction details and fire prevention, including finishes.
— Non-collusion certificate (optional).
— The form of tender (see 'Pro-forma letter of invitation to tender' and 'Pro-forma form of tender' below).
— Address to which tenders should be returned.
— Accompanying letter noting for example when the site can be inspected, confirming the tendering procedure (eg single-stage) and any other matters that need highlighting.

| 2. | Check that all necessary statutory and other consents have been obtained and that party wall awards are in place. If any permissions, consents or awards are still under negotiation during the tendering process this could mean that alterations will be required to the tender negotiations or that start on site will be delayed. |

| 3. | Discuss the list of potential contractors with the client and the design team. |

| 4. | If appropriate, arrange for interviews for selection of contractors by negotiation. |

| 5. | Confirm with the client: |

— The details of any phasing, restrictions and implications.
This activity might be carried out earlier in the process if it is fundamental to the design that construction is phased for financial or health and safety reasons – ie fire risk management on a refurbishment site.
— The details of any proposal for work not forming part of the Building Contract to be carried out by other persons.
— That arrangements for insurance for works, etc are being made.
— That he/she is aware of the requirements of insurance provisions in the Building Contract and that they appreciate the advisability of seeking specialist advice from their insurers or brokers.
It is very important that the client should be fully aware of the insurance requirements well in advance of the tender process.
— That the site will be available to the contractor on the date stated in the documents, and that there is nothing likely to prevent possession or commencement.
— Any intention to impose restrictions on the contractor's working methods (eg sequence, access, limitation on hours, noise). This could have an effect on the Technical Design and would be essential information for tenderers.
— The form of contract to be used.
— The tendering period and procedures to be followed in opening tenders and notifying results.

Allow adequate time for tendering, and for the assessment of tenders. The most acceptable tender must be thoroughly checked for errors, and this takes time. Allow time for checking by the principal designer.

— The appropriate choice for any optional provisions in the Building Contract. Advise on the particulars which need to be entered in the appendix to the Building Contract and referred to in the tender documents (eg dates, insurances, liquidated damages, option clauses).

— Any arrangements to employ persons direct to carry out work not forming part of the Building Contract during the contractor's occupation.

— The final tender list.

— That he/she has finalised all insurance arrangements.

— That the instruction to proceed has been given and confirmed in writing.

6.	Provide final information for pre-construction health and safety information and pass to the principal designer if applicable.

This should cover significant issues that a competent contractor would not normally be expected to be aware of through the design information.

7.	Check design team members' input to main contract tender documents for any inconsistencies or omissions.

8.	Make a final check to ascertain whether the selected firms have all completed the tendering questionnaire and any non-collusion or other similar certificates required by the client.

9.	If specialist subcontractors or suppliers are to be involved:

— Check that you have written confirmation from the client for inclusion of the firms proposed. Check willingness and availability of these firms and, if necessary, decide on additional names.

— Initiate tender action for quotations from specialist subcontractors and suppliers. When inviting tenders for specialist subcontract work that includes a design element, make certain that the client consents in writing, and that their interests are properly protected by warranty.

— Review quality management of potential suppliers and subcontractors and their general compliance in health and safety matters. Pass relevant information to the principal designer.

If the architect appoints a subcontractor for design work he/she is responsible for ensuring that the subcontractor complies with the CDM Regulations, even if they are an overseas company – for example a European door manufacturer.

— Review the tenders and accompanying information received from specialist subcontractors and suppliers with design team members.

— Refer all tenders to the cost consultant for cost checking. Approve specialist tenders and notify all tenderers of this decision.Refer all tenders to the cost consultant for cost checking. Approve specialist tenders and notify all tenderers of this decision.

— Ensure any CDP work is in the construction contract.

Follow the procedures stated in the main contract to be used for the appointment of specialist subcontractors. Only place advance orders with specialist subcontractors or suppliers as provided for in the subcontract documentation, and only if authorised in writing by the client.

Review the position with respect to advance orders for design, materials and fabrication by specialist subcontractors and suppliers, including named subcontractors. If authorised, take further necessary action. Always obtain authorisation before taking action on advance orders.

| 10. | Invite tenders for main contract works from contractors on the final tender list. |

— Follow the relevant codes of procedure for tendering to ensure fairness and reliable pricing. *Refer to the NBS Guide to Tendering for Construction Projects.*

— Supply all tenderers with identical information.

— If queries are raised during the tendering period, deal with them promptly, and notify all other tenderers in identical terms.

— Do not accept late tenders.

| 11. | Arrange for tenderers to have the opportunity to inspect the site and/or existing buildings during the tender period. |

12.	Appraise the tenders received with the cost consultant and prepare a report (or assist in preparing a report) with recommendations for the client:

— Check with the cost consultant for arithmetical errors in the most acceptable tender; if any are found, use the appropriate stated procedures.

— Inspect draft programmes submitted by tenderers, if required.

— If applicable arrange for the principal designer to inspect material submitted by tenderers relating to health and safety requirements, and to appraise the construction phase plan submitted in the most acceptable tender.

It may be appropriate for the principal designer to view this material from all tenderers, not just the most acceptable, as the health and safety content may make a submission unacceptable.

— Check that the tender includes information regarding the contractor's competency. Deal with tender errors, or the need for a reduction, strictly in accordance with recommended procedures.

13.	If the appointment includes Stage 6 Soft Landings activities, the architect must contribute to the appraisal of tenders/negotiations relative to the Handover Strategy and facilities management matters. If the appointment includes Post-occupancy Evaluation activities at Stages 6 and/or 7, the architect must identify any changes to targets and their causes.

14.	Prepare the tender report, review it with the client and discuss recommendations about acceptance.

Be wary of a very low tender and explain to the client the possible risks in accepting it.

15.	If the lowest figure is greater than the amount allowed for in the cost plan, discuss the most appropriate measures for reducing it with the cost consultant (such as making alterations to the design), agree the action to be taken with the client and initiate it through negotiation or re-tendering.

16.	Assist as necessary with any negotiations following consideration by the client of the most acceptable tender.

| 17. | Where there is a principal contractor, check with the client that a construction phase plan has been produced and that it is relevant and meets the requirements of the job. The plan should be project-specific, take into account the pre-construction information provided, and its contents should be proportionate to the site risks. |

| 18. | Notify the successful tenderer and arrange for signing of the contract documents. |

| 19. | Notify unsuccessful tenderers of the result when the Building Contract is signed, and provide figures when appropriate. |

Information exchange

| 1. | Finalised tender documents, which might include: |

— Drawings.
— Schedules.
— Bills of quantities/specifications/schedules of work.
— Pre-construction health and safety information.
— Terms of any bonds and warranties.
— Subcontractor information and tenders.

When sending out for tender, any of the following documents and information may be relevant:

— A list of all tender documents so that the tenderers can check they have received the complete package.
— Tender forms and details of procedure to be followed, eg type of tender required, submittals required, how the tender should be packaged and identified, to whom it should be sent.

- Site Information and surveys
- Drawings.
- Drawn schedules, eg for doors.
- Specification.
- Schedule of works.
- Schedule of rates.
- Activity schedule.
- Information release schedule.
- Pre-construction information.
- Programmed dates for proposed work.
- Details of any phased commencement or completion.
- Details of the Building Contract terms and conditions, including insurance provisions.
- Details of advance payment arrangements.
- Details of any bonds or guarantees required from the contractor or to be provided by the employer.
- Details of any warranties to be provided.
- Information prepared specially for use in self-build or semi-skilled operations.
- Information for issue to specialist subcontractors and suppliers in connection with tender invitations.
- Information which is not necessarily part of the tender package for use in dealings with third parties, landlords, tenants, funders, etc (eg in connection with leases, boundaries, party walls, etc).
- Outputs required after tenders have been received might include the following:
- Main contract tenders and report with recommendations.
- Tenders received from specialists with appropriate forms and numbered documents where appropriate.
- Signed contract.

> **Architect:**
> Laura Dewe Mathews

Date completed:
October 2012

Construction cost:
£245,000 (including
fees)

The 80m², one-bed, new-build house uses a cross-laminated timber superstructure, placed inside the existing perimeter brickwork walls and rising up out of them. The timber structure has been left exposed internally.

Externally the palette of materials is limited to the original brickwork, round 'fancy butt' western red cedar shingles and galvanised steel.

As both client and contract administrator, architect Laura Dewe Mathews used a JCT Homeowners contract. The main contractor was responsible for the project up to the completion of the shell. Dewe Mathews then oversaw the fit-out, employing various trades directly and completing some of the work personally.

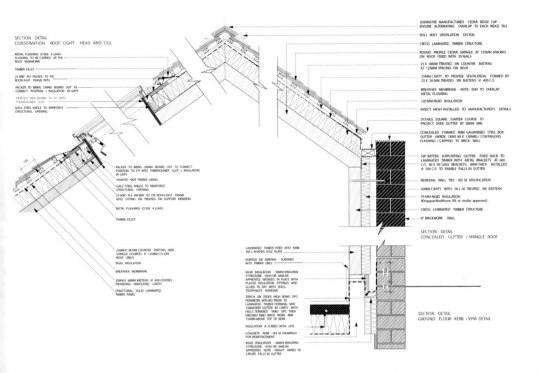

SECTION DETAIL
CONSERVATION ROOF LIGHT · HEAD AND CILL

METAL FLASHING (CODE 4 LEAD)
FLASHING TO BE CARRIED UP THE
ROOF 300MM MIN

TIMBER FILLET

25 WBP PLY PACKER TO FIX
ROOFLIGHT FRAME INTO

PACKER TO BRING LINING BOARD OUT TO
CORRECT POSITION + INSULATION IN GAPS

PAINTED MDF BOARD TO FIT INTO
THERMOLINER SLOT

GALV STEEL ANGLE TO REINFORCE
STRUCTURAL OPENING

PACKER TO BRING LINING BOARD OUT TO CORRECT
POSITION TO FIT INTO THERMOLINER SLOT + INSULATION
IN GAPS

PAINTED MDF TIMBER LINING

GALV STEEL ANGLE TO REINFORCE
STRUCTURAL OPENING

25 WBP PLY PACKER TO FIX ROOFLIGHT FRAME
INTO, SITTING ON TREATED SW SUPPORT MEMBERS

METAL FLASHING (CODE 4 LEAD)

TIMBER FILLET

25MM X 38 MM COUNTER BATTENS AND
SHINGLE COURSES @ 125MM C/S (ON
ROOF ONLY)

RIGID INSULATION

BREATHER MEMBRANE

25MM X 38MM BATTENS @ 400 CENTRES
PROVIDING VENTILATED CAVITY

STRUCTURAL SOLID LAMINATED
TIMBER PANEL

203MM PRE MANUFACTURED CEDAR RIDGE CAP ·
ENSURE ALTERNATING OVERLAP TO EACH RIDGE TILE

ROLL VENT VENTILATION SYSTEM

CROSS LAMINATED TIMBER STRUCTURE

ROUND PROFILE CEDAR SHINGLE AT 125MM SPACING
ON ROOF, FIXED WITH 55 NAILS

25 X 38MM TREATED SW COUNTER BATTENS
AT 125MM SPACING ON ROOF

25MM CAVITY TO PROVIDE VENTILATION, FORMED BY
25 X 38 MM TREATED SW BATTENS @ 400 C/S

BREATHER MEMBRANE - NOTE: END TO OVERLAP
METAL FLASHING

120 MM RIGID INSULATION

INSECT MESH INSTALLED TO MANUFACTURER'S DETAILS

DOUBLE SQUARE STARTER COURSE TO
PROJECT OVER GUTTER BY 38MM MIN

CONCEALED FORMED 3MM GALVANISED STEEL BOX
GUTTER (APPROX DIMS 80 X 120MM) / CONTINUOUS
FLASHING / CAPPING TO BRICK WALL

SW BATTEN SUPPORTING GUTTER, FIXED BACK TO
LAMINATED TIMBER WITH METAL BRACKETS AT 600
C/S, 90 X 90 GALV BRACKETS, 4MM THICK INSTALLED
@ 500 C/S TO ENABLE FALLS IN GUTTER

REMEDIAL WALL TIES - SEE SE SPECIFICATION

50MM CAVITY WITH 50 x 50 TREATED SW BATTENS

70 MM RIGID INSULATION
(Kingspan Kooltherm K8 or similar approved)

CROSS LAMINATED TIMBER STRUCTURE

9" BRICKWORK WALL

SECTION DETAIL
CONCEALED GUTTER / SHINGLE ROOF

LAMINATED TIMBER FIXED INTO KERB
VIA L-SHAPED SOLE PLATE

PAINTED SW SKIRTING - SCREWED
INTO TIMBER ONLY

RIGID INSULATION - 30MM KINGSPAN
STYROZONE H350 OR SIMILAR
APPROVED, WEDGED IN PLACE WITH
PLASTIC INSULATION FITTINGS AND
GLUED TO DPC WITH SHELL
TIXOZPHALTE ADHESIVE

TORCH ON ZEDEX HIGH BOND DPC,
PERIMETER APPLIED PRIOR TO
LAMINATED TIMBER FORMING MIN
75MM DEEP GUTTER IN CAVITY WITH
FALLS TOWARDS YARD. DPC THEN
DRESSED INTO BRICK WORK MIN
150MM ABOVE TOP OF KERB

INSULATION & SCREED WITH UFH

CONCRETE KERB - SEE SE DRAWINGS
FOR REINFORCEMENT

RIGID INSULATION - 30MM KINGSPAN
STYROZONE H350 OR SIMILAR
APPROVED. NOTE : HEIGHT VARIES TO
CREATE FALLS IN GUTTER

SECTION DETAIL
GROUND FLOOR KERB / VPM DETAIL

Awards:
Winner – Architects
Journal Small Projects
Award 2013, Winner
– Grand Designs Small
Projects Award 2013
Shortlisted – New
London Awards 2013

Form of contract:
JCT Homeowner

Due to the use of the cross-laminated timber, the 12-week lead time, and the permissions required from the local council (to erect the CLT superstructure using a crane, requiring a road closure), the main contractor was under pressure to complete all preparatory work on time and to a high tolerance. This included all below-ground drainage, foundations, slab and vapour-proof membrane. This pressure ensured good progress on site prior to the arrival of the CLT. The design coordination required for the bespoke galvanised steel flashings, gutters and window reveals did however cause delays later on in the project, although with foresight the time involved should have been anticipated. These delays were eclipsed by the time taken to complete the fit-out, which had to take place once the house was partially inhabited.

The result is a small yet generously proportioned house. At ground floor level it retains the openness of the original workshop yet has a sense of separation from the adjacent street.

Project issues

Contractor Procurement options

There are a number of methods of contractor Procurement that can be followed, depending on which of the three criteria of time, quality and cost are the more important. The principal options are as follows:

Traditional Procurement
Tendering involves the assembly and coordination of the Developed Design and Technical Design information into the tender package. This is the most prevalent form for small projects.

Design and build Procurement
In design and build Procurement, tendering activities may occur at different points in the Plan of Work. In cases where the client wishes to tender on detailed information, the stages may follow something close to the normal sequence, but in others, where the design and build contract is entered into on minimal information, tendering may follow Stage 2, with Stages 3 and 4 occurring after the Building Contract is let.

Design and Build is unusual in small projects but may be appropriate in certain cases, and the JCT Minor Works Building Contract has a 'with contractor's design' version (see Procurement: Construction contracts below).

Management Procurement
With management procurement, the amount of Technical Design information available at the commencement of the project will be limited to the extent that much of the detailed information will be supplied by the works contractors in the form of shop or installation drawings. Nevertheless, the general Technical Design information will originate from the design team, and the process of coordinating and integrating information will continue throughout the construction of the project.

Management procurement can be appropriate for certain small projects where price is not a key criterion.

A further option identified in the RIBA Plan of Work 2013 is contractor-led procurement although this is unlikely to be used on small projects.

Tendering procedure

Tenders for small projects will generally include three to five pre-selected parties. Where price is not the main criterion they may be negotiated.

It is important to ensure that tendering is always carried out on a fair basis. Competition should only be between firms which have the necessary skills, integrity, responsibility and reputation to enable them to deliver work of the nature and standard required. Competitive tendering should involve only a realistic number of bids from firms that have been given the same information and the same realistic period in which to formulate offers. It is sound practice always to follow current relevant guidance, and reference should be made to the *NBS Guide to Tendering: for Construction Projects* (2011).

Key principles of good practice to be adopted when appointing zcontractors are as follows:

Clear procedures should be followed that ensure fair and transparent competition in a single round of tendering consisting of one or more stages.

The tender process should ensure compliant, competitive tenders.

Tender lists should be compiled systematically from a number of qualified contractors.

Tender lists should be as short as possible.

Conditions should be the same for all tenderers.

Confidentiality should be respected by all parties.

Sufficient time should be given for the preparation and evaluation of tenders.

Sufficient information should be given for the preparation of tenders.

Tenders should be assessed and accepted on quality as well as price.

Working practices that avoid or discourage collusion should be followed.

Suites of contracts and standard unamended forms of contract from recognised bodies should be used where they are available used to set out matters related to the tendering process.

If you are using an NBS specification there are preliminary clauses that can be used to set out matters related to the tendering process.

Establishing a tender list

Many practices maintain a list of contractors with a note of size/turnover, sectors covered, location, previous performance and so on for use in preparing a preliminary tender list, and this can be a useful, timesaving device. It is important to keep it up to date and to keep an eye out for appropriate new additions.

Assessing tenders and notification

It is important to follow a clear and open procedure throughout the process. Determine what the criteria will be before tender invitations are sent out and always include quality criteria as well as cost and programme.

Tenders should be dealt with in a timely manner and opened as soon as possible after the date of receipt, and it is good practice to notify unsuccessful tenderers what the other bids were (without disclosing which contractor submitted which price).

You should decide before going to tender how pricing errors will be dealt with – either the tenderer will be given the opportunity to confirm or withdraw, or amend the price for it then to be re-compared to the other offers received.

If the lowest tender is above the client's budget or they are all unacceptable for other reasons, the client will have to do one of the following:

— Increase the budget.
— Negotiate a reduction in the tender by amending the design or specification.
— Re-tender with an amended design or specification.

Clearly if redesign is required this will attract additional design/consultancy fees which will need to be negotiated. This should not occur if the cost consultant has maintained a cost plan leading up to tender.

Standard letters for tendering

Preliminary invitation to tender

Project name and address

Dear [name]

We are preparing a preliminary list of tenderers for construction of the works described below. Please confirm whether you wish to be invited to submit a tender for these works. Your acceptance will confirm your agreement to submit a bona fide tender and not divulge your tender price to any person or body before the time for submission of tenders. Once the contract has been let, we aim to supply all tenderers with a list of the tender prices.

Please reply by [date]. Your inclusion in the preliminary list at this stage will not guarantee that you will receive a formal invitation to tender for these works.

Yours faithfully,

[name]

For and on behalf of [company name]

a. Job:
b. Employer:
c. Architect/contract administrator:
d. Cost consultant:
e. Other consultants:
f. Location of site (site plan enclosed):
g. General description of work:
h. Approximate cost range £_____ to £_____
i. Form of contract:
j. Anticipated date for possession:
k. Period for completion of the works:
l. Approximate date for issue of tender documents:
m. Tender period _____ weeks
n. Tender to remain open for _____ weeks
o. Liquidated damages (if any), anticipated value £____ per ____
p. Particular conditions applying to the contract:

Invitation to tender

Project name and address

Dear [name]

Following your acceptance to the invitation to tender for the above we are pleased to enclose the following:

Technical information as set out on the accompanying drawing issue sheet [to include all plans, sections, elevations, details, diagrams, specifications, schedules and so on; send 2 copies if posted]

The form of tender [send 2 copies if posted]

Copies of the relevant advance orders [if applicable]

The completed form of tender is to be returned to the above address/emailed to [add email address]*
by [date].

Please acknowledge receipt of this email/letter* and enclosed information and confirm that you are able to submit a tender in accordance with these instructions.

Yours faithfully,
[name]

For and on behalf of [company name]

* Delete as applicable

Response

We have read the conditions of contract and have examined the Technical Design information issued to us. We offer to execute and complete, in accordance with the conditions of contract, the whole of the works described for the sum of:

£_____.__ (and in words) _____

Within ____ weeks from the date of possession of the site.

This tender remains open for ____ days from the date set for submitting tenders.

Letter to successful tenderer

We are pleased to inform you that your tender for these works is acceptable and we will be in touch shortly to make arrangements for you to sign the contract.

Letter to unsuccessful tenderer

Tenders were opened on [date]. We regret to inform you that your tender was not successful. This will not affect your opportunity to tender for work through us in the future.

The full list of tenderers and prices is below:

Tenderers (in alphabetical order):
....
....

Prices (in descending order):
....
....

Construction contracts

The RIBA has developed two new contracts to cover matters not properly covered by existing contracts. The forms are:

Domestic Building Contract

Concise Building Contract

RIBA Domestic Building Contract

The RIBA Domestic Building Contract has been developed to provide a simple yet comprehensive contract solution for building works at a client's home. It is suitable for all types of domestic works including simple renovations and also more complex extensions and new buildings. The contract uses optional clauses to cover more advanced contractual terms therefore retaining its simplicity.

The trend has been to use a commercial construction contract (because of its more comprehensive terms) for works at a client's home. This practice requires that some of the terms of such contracts are individually negotiated with the consumer client; failure to keep to this requirement could lead to misunderstanding and expensive disputes. The RIBA Domestic Building Contract is comprehensive, covering issues not provided for by other domestic contracts including programme, liquidated damages, testing and rejection of defective works among others and it is written in plain English for the consumer to understand and therefore it should not require individual negotiation of its terms.

Also, some of the terms in commercial construction contracts may distract rather than facilitate the successful completion of works at the client's home, an example of such term is the detailed payment procedure required under the law for commercial construction projects. The RIBA Domestic Contract provides terms that are suitable and aid the successful completion of works at the client's home and cover recurrent issues that arise in such projects, these include:

flexible payment terms covering payment on completion, periodic payment and payment on achieving set milestones, an option for insurance backed guarantee to cover the customer in the event the contractor ceases to trade,

collaboration that is not complicated but allows the parties to work together effectively, including over events that may delay completion or add costs to the Works,

emphasis on timely completion of the works including specifying time limits for the contractor to make applications for extension of time and additional payment,

gives the contractor the right to apply for payment protecting the contractor against late payment.

The publishers of the contract have advised that other benefits of the contract include:

Provides an effective but not onerous clause for the contractor to provide a programme showing the sequence it intends to carry out the works and to update the programme regularly,

provision for the client to specify suppliers or sub-contractors of its choice without changing the balance of liabilities between the parties,

provision for the Contractor to design parts of the building works with comprehensive terms covering insurance and contractor's intellectual property rights,

completion in sections,

straightforward method for dealing with changes in a project within agreed timescales

comprehensive insurance provisions to offer the client peace of mind.

RIBA Concise Building Contract

The RIBA Concise Building Contract is the commercial version of the RIBA contracts. It is suitable for all types of small and minor commercial building work. It is written in plain English for easy understanding.

The contract is concise and relatively shorter than other commercial forms. The contract uses optional clauses to offer more advanced contractual terms while retaining its simplicity.

The publishers of the contract advice that the contract improves on existing contracts, such improvements include:

Provides for effective collaboration between the parties focusing on areas that have historically created disputes,

Gives parties better mechanism to ensure the timely completion of the building project by setting out a straightforward process for dealing with changes to the project within specified timescales,

Gives the contract administrator comprehensive powers to administer the contract including the power to visit off site locations in relation to the works, instruct that works that has been covered up, be uncovered, power to reject defective work and also power to accept a defect and amend the Contract Price accordingly,

It does not contain unnecessary administrative procedures for instance a Certificate of Non-Completion; it is developed to aid the effective administration of the project and provides a clear process for dealing with defects that are identified after Practical completion.

The Contract payment provisions comply with Housing Grants, Regeneration and Construction act as amended by Local democracy economic development and construction Act 2009 (Construction Act as amended). However, the contract also provides payment options for projects lasting for less than 45 days and therefore not required to comply with the stringent provisions of the Construction Act as amended.

The publishers have advised that other benefits include:

Provides an effective but not onerous provision for the contractor to submit a programme showing the sequence it intends to carry out the works and to update the programme regularly,

Allows for completion in sections,

Provides for Contractor to design parts of the works with comprehensive terms covering insurance and contractor's intellectual property rights,

Allows the Employer to specify suppliers or sub-contractors of their choice without changing the balance of liability between the parties,

Provides a mechanism for advanced payment and repayment of the advanced payment sum,

Provides a collateral warranty/ third party agreement clause to secure the rights of funders and future purchasers or tenants,

Allow the parties the option to set out rules to govern applications for revision of time or extra payments.

RIBA Construction Contracts online

RIBA have also developed an easy to use online version of the contracts. The online RIBA contracts allow parties to alter, manage and view the contracts online before printing the final contract. Being an internet based service with adequate security; it represents forward thinking in the contract management and negotiation process.

The other standard forms of contract that can be used on small projects are:

JCT Intermediate IC11 (in two forms: with and without contractor's design)

JCT Minor Works MW11 (in two forms: with and without contractor's design)

JCT Building Contract for a Homeowner/Occupier (in two forms: with and without an associated consultancy agreement)

Intermediate contracts

IC11 can be used where subcontractors are to be named (ie the contractor required to subcontract to a specific contractor or supplier) and where sectional completion is required. It is suitable for contract periods of up to 12 months (although this is a rough guide only) and a contract sum of £1m would be acceptable provided the work is 'of a simple content' and 'without any building service installations of a complex nature'.

Care should be taken where the client is a homeowner (consumer) as individual negotiation may be required prior to the contract being entered into.

Minor Works contracts

The MW contracts are by some margin the most commonly used and are appropriate for projects:

Up to around £250,000 and no more than six months' duration.

Where the work involved is simple in character.

Where the work is designed by or on behalf of the employer.

Where the employer is to provide drawings and/or a specification and/or work schedules to define adequately the quantity and quality of the work.

Where a contract administrator is to administer the conditions.

Where the contractor is to design discrete part(s) of the works, even though all the other criteria are met, you should use the contractor's design (MWD) version.

As with the Intermediate form, care should be taken where the client is a homeowner (consumer) as individual negotiation may be required prior to the contract being entered into.

Homeowner contracts

The Homeowner form is a consumer contract for residential occupiers, written in plain English to comply with the Unfair Terms in Consumer Contracts Regulations 1999. It is only nine pages long, comprising a page for the customer's (client's) and the contractor's contact details, four pages for the 'arrangements' for the works and four pages for the conditions. There are two versions; one for use where the homeowner/occupier has not appointed a consultant to oversee the work (HO/B) and the other where a consultant has been appointed to oversee the work (HO/C + HO/CA).

HO/B is appropriate:

For small domestic building work such as extensions and alterations.

Where the proposed works are to be carried out for an agreed lump sum.

Where no consultant acts on behalf of the homeowner/occupier to administer the contract.

The HO/B pack contains:

Building Contract for a homeowner/occupier who has not appointed a consultant to oversee the work (two copies – one each for the customer and the contractor).

Enquiry letter (a sample for sending to potential contractors).

Guidance notes.

HO/C is appropriate:

For small domestic building work such as extensions and alterations.

Where the proposed works are to be carried out for an agreed lump sum.

Where detailed procedures are not required.

Where the homeowner/occupier has appointed a consultant who will be administering the contract for the homeowner/occupier.

The HO/C pack contains:

Building Contract for a homeowner/occupier who has appointed a consultant to oversee the work (two copies – one each for the customer and the contractor).

Consultancy agreement (HO/CA) for a homeowner/occupier appointing a consultant to provide consultancy services in relation to building work (two copies – one each for the customer and the consultant).

Guidance notes.

Published as part of the Building Contract and consultancy agreement for a homeowner/occupier, this agreement is for use between the homeowner/occupier and the consultant (eg architect, engineer or surveyor) on who is to provide services. It covers a range of services that the consultant can provide, such as producing designs and detailed specifications for the work, applying for planning permission and Building Regulations approval, and inspecting the building work while it is being done.

The agreement is designed for use with the Building Contract for a homeowner/occupier who has appointed a consultant. It may however be used independently of this contract but care must be taken to ensure it is compatible.

A construction contract with a residential occupier or someone who intends to occupy the dwelling as his/her residence is excluded from the provisions of the Housing Grants, Construction and Regeneration Act 1996; nevertheless this contract provides for adjudication in the event of a dispute between the homeowner/occupier and the consultant.

Neither the HO/B nor the HO/C is suitable for use in Scotland. Separate versions are published and issued by the Scottish Building Contract Committee Limited (SBCC) for use in Scotland.

For detailed advice on contracts refer to the RIBA guides available through www.ribabookshops.com.

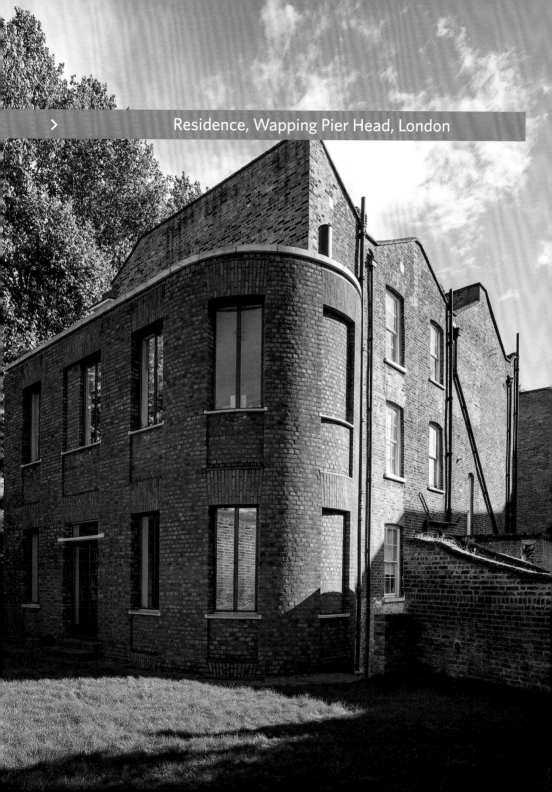

Before

> **Architect:**
Chris Dyson
Architects

Date completed:
May 2013

Construction cost:
£442,000

Awards:
Winner – Architects'
Journal Small
Projects Award 2014

This Grade II Listed end-of-terrace house was owned by the London Borough of Tower Hamlets and, until 2008, operated as a nunnery. The property was then vacant, suffering from subsidence and dilapidation, and pronounced unsafe to occupy. The Council marketed the house for sale by sealed bids and bidders were requested to provide an offer which included a design proposal for bringing the property back into habitable use.

The brief was to create a private family home for now and the foreseeable future; to undertake not just the necessary work but to recreate a sense of character that had been lost over the last 50 years.

The architect proposed an enlarged three-storey extension (including basement) to replace the condemned Victorian extension. A curved rear facade addressed the garden, and the gross internal area was increased from 154m² to 248m².

248

The appointment was through a bespoke letter (modelled on the RIBA Domestic Project Agreement 2010) covering all RIBA work stages.

The client priorities were expressed as early mobilisation, quality craftsmanship and good value. The architect introduced them to a trusted construction team with whom they had worked with frequently. A project manager was appointed to coordinate the individual contractors, all of whom were employed on a direct labour basis. This dramatically reduced costs associated with preliminaries and contract administration and meant that the project relied greatly on trust and working relationships between contractors.

Practice issues

Building and maintaining a supply chain

Many small practices maintain lists of contractors and other consultants with whom they regularly work and have a good understanding. For new practices it is sensible to start keeping such a list. Ask other practices to tell you about their preferred contractors and suppliers and be prepared to share your ideas with them. Use a spreadsheet similar to the one set out under CRM in Stage 7, above.

All practices, but particularly micro practices, can benefit from collaborating with others and outsourcing work they either do not have the skills, time or resources to undertake. Meet with other practices in your area and get an understanding of what they can do, and discern whether you feel you could form a working relationship with them. Consider what you could offer them, and look to fill gaps in your expertise. This exercise is also one that will benefit from maintaining a record in spreadsheet format.

You can also consider forming more formal relationships to address new markets and to allow you to pitch to clients with a broader portfolio. Make sure there is a clear memorandum of understanding between you and your collaborators, so that when projects do arise there is no misunderstanding about who will be doing what and how fees will be allocated. Make sure the arrangement brings benefits for both parties, so that the investment you make in getting it going is repaid. Collaboration on a series of projects will help improve working practices and drive efficiency.

> ## Stage Summary

Getting the right contractor – rather than just the cheapest – requires a well-managed tender process but is time well-spent. The alternative is having a poor or inexperienced contractor, which is likely to lead to poor-quality execution of the project and wasted time and resources.

Set up procedures that can be followed on other projects, but make sure that each one is reviewed on its merits and a suitable Procurement route followed that suits its particular needs.

Allow enough time for contractor mobilisation in the overall programme and be prepared to wait for the right contractor if time is not the most critical factor.

Section IV

On Site

Introduction

Architects are going to increasingly be bidding and competing for work as members of teams: developers, contractors, designers, all coming together to deliver.

David Partridge, Argent

Stages 5 and 6 have been grouped together in this book, reflecting the fact that the Defects Liability Period (DLP) element of Stage 6 is generally a necessary part of completing the contract administration and the Soft Landings element should commence during the DLP. POE is usually undertaken under a separate contract.

Stage 5 can be the most rewarding part of the project – to see the design realised – but it can also be the most risky. The construction stage will generally run smoothly if the Technical Design information produced during Stage 4 is sound. Usually on small projects it will be the same person who is responsible for both stages. However pressure on fees and a lack of Technical Design experience can lead to insufficient time being spent on Stage 4 with consequent issues arising. One of the most important messages in this book is to allow enough time and resources to complete the Technical Design work to the very best of your ability. Do not cut corners as this will almost inevitably lead to additional work during construction, the possibility of contractor-led variations and the potential for consequent legal action from the client.

For some, the technical side of building design is the most interesting and rewarding. For others it can be a challenge and practices should consider carefully whether they would prefer to undertake work only up to Stage 3, with others taking on the work from there. This approach has the significant disadvantage of losing control over the all-important detail and consequently the quality of the end product.

One solution for those who are daunted by the technical and contractual end of projects is to collaborate with other practices who specialise in this but are less able to deliver the earlier, more creative work during Stages 1–3. Our profession operates in a time where there is arguably more to know than one person can alone, and for the many micro practices and sole practitioners who undertake small projects some form of collaboration is worth considering.

Stage 5

Construction

RIBA Plan of Work 2013 Stage 5

RIBA
Plan of
Work
2013

Stage 5

Construction

Task Bar	Tasks
Core Objectives	Offsite manufacturing and onsite **Construction** in accordance with the **Construction Programme** and resolution of **Design Queries** from site as they arise.
Procurement Variable task bar	Administration of **Building Contract**, including regular site inspections and review of progress.
Programme Variable task bar	*The RIBA Plan of Work 2013 enables this stage to overlap with a number of other stages depending on the selected procurement route.*
(Town) Planning Variable task bar	*There are no specific activities in the RIBA Plan of Work 2013, however the contractor will need to comply with any construction-specific planning conditions, such as monitoring of noise levels.*
Suggested Key Support Tasks	Review and update **Sustainability Strategy** and implement **Handover Strategy**, including agreement of information required for commissioning, training, handover, asset management, future monitoring and maintenance and ongoing compilation of **'As-constructed' Information**. Update **Construction** and **Health and Safety Strategies**. *Support tasks are now focused on health and safety on site and ensuring that the project handover and post-occupancy activities, determined earlier, are properly facilitated.*
Sustainability Checkpoints	• *Has the design stage sustainability assessment been certified?* • *Have sustainability procedures been developed with the contractor and included in the* **Construction Strategy**? • *Has the detailed commissioning and* **Handover Strategy** *programme been reviewed?* • *Confirm that the contractor's interim testing and monitoring of construction has been reviewed and observed, particularly in relation to airtightness and continuity of insulation.* • *Is the non-technical user guide complete and the aftercare service set up?* • *Has the* **'As-constructed' Information** *been issued for post-construction sustainability certification?*
Information Exchanges (at stage completion)	**'As-constructed' Information.**
UK Government Information Exchanges	Not required.

Introduction

Stage 5 maps to the former Stage K (Construction to Practical Completion) but also includes Stage J (Mobilisation).

For the project leader, subject to the form of construction contract and terms of the appointment, this stage can involve:

— Administration of the Building Contract.
— Making regular inspections of the work on site.
— Certifying stage payments.

Along with Stage 4, the activities during this stage are the ones associated with the highest level of risk, both in terms of the amount of work in relation to the fee and in terms of things going wrong! It is generally an area that practitioners must undertake both to ensure the quality of the end product and because it is generally expected by clients. It is however something that should only be undertaken by those who feel they have the core technical and managerial experience and necessary skills.

This section of the book provides some key advice to help keep you out of trouble during this stage of a project. A thorough and well-considered set of tender and construction information prepared during Stage 4 will have gone a long way to achieving that.

It is not unusual for further technical information to be developed after Stage 5 has commenced but this should be considered a Stage 4 activity where Stages 4 and 5 overlap. However, information produced in response to site queries is a Stage 5 activity.

Project activities

Information required

1.	Building Contract, with all necessary entries and supplements, ready for completion by the parties.
2.	Contract documents, including drawings and specifications/schedules of work.
3.	Completed tender documents from the successful tenderer.
4.	Written records of any post-tender changes to the contracted project.
5.	Administration forms suitable for the form of Building Contract to be used.
6.	Contractor's rates or contract sum analysis if appropriate, and/or specifications/schedules of work.
7.	Specialists' tenders and documents ready for nomination instructions to be issued.
8.	Contractor's master programme.
9.	When applicable, copies of the construction phase plan developed by the contractor.
10.	Copies of any method statements prepared by the contractor as required in the Building Contract conditions.
11.	Information release schedule, or schedule agreed with the contractor indicating what further information is needed from the architect (and by when), or verification by the contractor, if applicable, that all necessary information has been supplied, and accepting that any further drawings will be their own responsibility.

Stage activities

1.	In the event of an omission or a substitution necessitating revisions to detail design, take appropriate action if authorised by the client. Alert the client to any additional costs, fees or alterations to the Project Programme.
2.	Check that all unsuccessful tenderers have been properly notified.
3.	Remind the client of their responsibility for the building in terms of insurance, security and maintenance.
4.	Compile a directory of all parties involved in the construction stage.
5.	If the appointment includes Soft Landings activities under Stage 6, the architect must: — Discuss the initial occupation provisions specified in the Building Contract with the contractor. — Review design information from the contractor or specialists for compliance with occupation and facilities management strategies. — Review and monitor the contractor's building readiness programme. — Prepare the building's user guide and contribute to periodic reports. — Agree the timing and scope of Soft Landings activities. If the appointment includes Post-occupancy Evaluation activities under Stage 6, the architect must: — Discuss the specified review provisions with the contractor. — Identify any changes to targets, and their causes, and contribute to periodic reports.
6.	If applicable, remind the client of relevant statutory obligations under the CDM Regulations relating to the role of the principal designer and the competence of the principal contractor and other contractor's performance in health and safety matters. If applicable, remind the client of the requirement for a health and safety file to be deposited in a safe place at the completion of the project.

7.	Check that any necessary approvals and consents have been obtained and are on file. If any are still outstanding, explain to the client the consequences of starting on site prematurely. It is wise to draw up an approvals and conditions tracker that identifies when and how each is discharged.
8.	Check with the client that all necessary party wall awards are in place.
9.	Check the scope of professional services agreed with the client for continued presence of the design team members as members of the project team.
10.	Agree the scope and timetable for any amendments needed to Building Contract documents as a result of post-tender negotiations.
11.	Convene and chair site progress meetings or attend progress meetings chaired by the contractor. Keep accurate minutes of meetings, and record discussions, progress statements and decisions.
12.	Confirm that consultants are to supply relevant information for the preparation of operating instructions, maintenance manuals, record drawings of installation, etc.
13.	Where required, confirm that consultants are to carry out detailed inspection of specialist work and report to the architect. If authorised, consultants should also attend commissioning, testing and witnessing and report. Identify responsibility for commissioning, testing and witnessing of engineering services and ensure that they are carried out according to the provisions of the Building Contract.
14.	Review and update the Sustainability Strategy.
15.	Review implementation of the Handover Strategy, including agreement of information required for commissioning, training, handover, asset management, future monitoring and maintenance and ongoing compilation of 'As-constructed' Information.
16.	Update the Health and Safety Strategy.

| 17. | Check that information relating to the health and safety file and operating and maintenance manuals is complete and ready for handing over to the principal designer. |

| 18. | Confirm the programme and procedures for site visits. |

Visit the site as provided for in the agreement with the client, whether for periodic checks, predictive checks or spot checks, to observe and comment on the contractor's site supervision and examples of work.

Keep methodical records of all site visits and results of all tests witnessed or reported. Allow adequate time on site to carry out checks properly. Make careful notes and compile a systematic record of visits. It helps to prepare checklists relating to the stage of the work. Check that work is being executed generally in accordance with the provisions of the Building Contract, in a proper and workmanlike manner and in accordance with the health and safety plan.

| 19. | If appointed as information manager, for any residual detailed design activities occurring at this stage: |

— Assist members of the design team to develop the design using the BIM model, ensuring that data-sharing protocols are followed.
— Check and sign off the model at agreed stages.
— Issue or assist in the issue of design data at agreed times throughout the development of the design.
— Assist in the development of data relative to the agreed levels of detail.
— Assist in the integration of contractor's, subcontractors' and suppliers' data into the BIM model.
— Coordinate and release 'end of construction' BIM record model data at the appropriate time.

If appointed as contract administrator

| 1. | Explain the conditions of the contract to the client/employer and in particular the requirement to make stage payments in accordance with any valuations made or certificates issued. |

| 2. | Prepare Building Contract documents for signature. Send by registered/recorded post or deliver by hand. It is customary to send these first to the contractor and then to the employer. When preparing Building Contract documents for signature or completion as a deed, check that entries are correct and relate to the tender documents. If there is more than one copy, check that they are identical. |

| 3. | Check: |

— That both parties have properly signed the Building Contract documents and that any agreed alterations are initialled.

— That additional copies of drawings and other documents are handed to the main contractor as required by the Building Contract.

— Bonds and warranties required from the contractor. These should be obtained before the Building Contract is signed.

Note: for commercial projects it is the client's duty to ensure that construction does not start until the principal contractor has prepared an appropriate construction phase plan and made arrangements for suitable welfare facilities to be present from the start of the work.

— Quality management proposals and procedures with the contractor.

— Proposed site planning and accommodation with the contractor.

— With the client that the Building Contract documents have been completed and signed as a simple contract or a deed as applicable.

— The contractor's insurance policies and pass on to the employer for checking by their brokers or insurance advisers. Check original documents carefully for cover and renewal dates.

— The contractor's programmes and confirm information schedules.

| 4. | If possible, named subcontractors should be appointed at the commencement of the Building Contract, always strictly in accordance with stipulated procedures. Note the subcontract dates for compatibility with the main contractor's programme. |

| 5. | Provide the contractor with copies of contract documents as required under the Building Contract. |

6.	Hold a pre-contract meeting with the Project Team and issue minutes as appropriate.
7.	Check that the contractor is working according to the Construction Programme and report to the employer on this. The contractor will be expected to review progress against the Construction Programme and annotate the programme accordingly.
8.	Monitor the contractor's compliance with planning conditions.
9.	Remind the client that instructions to the contractor can only be issued by way of a contract administrator's instruction, and advise the client of the employer's obligations under the Building Contract, and of the role and duties of the architect in administering the Building Contract.
10.	Confirm that all instructions concerning specialist subcontractors or suppliers are to be channelled through the contract administrator, to be included under a contract administrator's instruction issued to the main contractor.
11.	Confirm with the client and cost consultant the procedures for valuation and certification. Report to the client on cost matters at agreed intervals.
12.	Confirm dates for commencement and completion.
13.	Clarify any queries from the contractor.
14.	Arrange for the handover of site and/or existing buildings, allowing the contractor exclusive possession or to the extent previously agreed.
15.	Meet the contractor on site to note setting out, including boundaries, fencing and hoardings, amenities and welfare arrangements, protective measures, etc to establish compliance with the contractor's method statements and the requirements of the Building Contract.

| 16. | Administer the Building Contract in accordance with the procedural rules and the conditions, acting fairly and impartially between the parties. |

Issue contract administrator's instructions, discretionary or obligatory, as empowered under the Building Contract and in accordance with the contract provisions.

Note that any design changes may have health and safety implications, and the designer should involve the principal designer in any decisions where the variation has such an impact. It is good practice to keep the principal designer in the loop on instructions and variations as it helps him/her to keep track of information that could be useful for the health and safety file.

Provide the client with estimates of costs arising from the contract administrator's instructions, including variations.

Note:
— *All instructions to the contractor should be in writing: it is good practice to issue them on a contract administrator's instruction form (not via correspondence or site meeting minutes).*
— *Only empowered instructions should be issued: keep the wording concise and unambiguous.*
— *Confirm oral instructions as soon as necessary to avoid difficulties and to ensure that construction cost estimates are realistic.*

| 17. | Provide information as set out in the information release schedule, or provide additional necessary information to the contractor as required under the provisions of the Building Contract. |

It is important to ensure that there is no reasonably necessary information outstanding, general or specific.

| 18. | Inspect the contractor's progress measured against the Construction Programme, and generally inspect goods and materials delivered to the site. |

19.	Deal with claims as empowered under the terms of the Building Contract.

Variations should be pre-priced if possible, otherwise the likely full implications should be estimated and agreed before action is taken. It may be that negotiation is the best way forward, but do not exceed your authority.

Beware of claims regarding matters not dealt with under the express terms of the Building Contract because the contract administrator has no power to settle these; they must be dealt with between the parties. Issue instructions with respect to provisional sums and the appointment of specialist subcontractors, etc.

20.	Issue certificates as authorised and required in accordance with the Building Contract procedures.

Be punctilious about valuations and certificates for payment.

Notify the cost consultant in writing of any work not properly carried out, so that such work is not included in any valuation.

Notify the cost consultant of any work against which monies must be withheld or where 'an appropriate deduction' is to be made from the contract sum.

Alert the client to any rights to make a deduction from the amount certified, and the procedures involved.

21.	Initiate pre-completion checks on the works and make records of outstanding items.

Note: any lists are for the benefit of the design team and the client, and not normally for issue to the contractor. Under JCT traditional forms, quality control on site, snagging, etc are entirely the responsibility of the contractor.

22.	When completion is near, make sure that the contractor is fully aware that commissioning must be completed and operating manuals available before the building is handed over.

The principal designer must pass the H&S file to the principal contractor to complete and then hand to the client. However if the principal designer's appointment continues up to practical completion then the principal designer will pass the completed H&S file directly to the client.

23.	Issue the certificate of Practical Completion in accordance with the provisions of the Building Contract. Certify Practical Completion only when, in your opinion, this state has been attained.

Be wary of pressure from the contractor or client to certify Practical Completion early – the consequences can be serious for all concerned.

Information exchange after mobilisation

1.	Documentation setting out agreed adjustments to the tender figure, if relevant, to arrive at an acceptable contract figure.
2.	Building Contract documents duly signed and initialled as appropriate by the employer and contractor as parties to the contract.
3.	Requisite sets of drawings, schedules and other documents for issue to the main contractor.
4.	Approved tenders and documents in respect of specialist subcontractors for issue to the main contractor.
5.	Construction phase plan and HSE notification.

Note: F10 notification is undertaken by the client, but the principal contractor must display a copy of this F10 on the site.

Information exchange after construction

1.	'As-constructed' Information from the contractor.
2.	Record copies of correspondence, information, decisions and instructions, valuations and certificates, as necessary for the contractor to perform their obligations under the Building Contract, issued during the progress of the works.
3.	Manuals or other maintenance information required under the Building Contract.
4.	Health and safety file information, as required under the CDM Regulations, if applicable.
5.	Programmes for maintenance, if required.

Sustainability Checkpoint 5

With the design work complete the majority of activities at this stage are in relation to ensuring that the commissioning and handover activities agreed during Stage 1 are properly implemented.

Sustainability aims

The main aim is to ensure that the Sustainability Strategy underpinning the design is carried through into construction, and to manage the handover in a way that will ensure that the client can operate the building as intended on occupation.

Key actions

1.	Pass the Site Waste Management Plan to the contractor.
2.	Design stage sustainability assessment to be certified.
3.	Develop construction sustainability procedures with the contractor.
4.	Review the commissioning and handover programme.
5.	Review and observe the contractor's interim testing and monitoring of construction, particularly airtightness and continuity of insulation.
6.	Review the implications of changes to the specification or design against agreed sustainability criteria.
7.	Complete the non-technical user guide and aftercare service set-up.
8.	Assist with collating as-built information for post-construction sustainability certification.

9.	Collaborate with the contractor to maximise construction phase potential to meet sustainability criteria as economically as possible.
10.	Submit final information for statutory approval and certification, including Building Regulations Part L submission and energy performance certificates (EPC).
11.	Visit the site to check that quality, installation, etc are in line with sustainability targets.
12.	Review the content of the operating and maintenance manual with the facilities manager, who should sign it off when it is complete and acceptable.
13.	Stress the importance of design elements that are essential to meeting sustainability targets and how to monitor whether they are operating correctly.
14.	Work with the client's facilities managers to ensure a smooth handover, with all records finalised and coordinated and with adequately trained operating and maintenance staff in place ahead of completion.
15.	Check that adequate maintenance contracts are in place and that they will commence immediately after handover.
16.	Confirm responsibilities and routines for data recording to monitor performance and assist in fine tuning.
17.	Identify aftercare representative(s) and when they will be available on site.

Before

After

Architect:
Chris Dyson Architects

Date completed:
May 2012

Construction cost:
£257,000

Awards:
Finalist - AJ Retrofit
Awards (2014)

This residential project is a Victorian semi-detached building located within a conservation area in South London. The proposal was to rationalise the existing ground floor layout of this late nineteenth-century house to create a space which suits twenty-first-century living. The existing kitchen was retained with the removal of the adjacent utility room to create a large, open-plan kitchen, dining and living area. The small extension to the rear and side of the property integrates floor-to-ceiling 'frameless' glazing to create a space in direct contact with the garden.

During Stage 2, a Thames Water drainage and water search indicated a drain to the rear of the property. Prior to work commencing on-site a CCTV survey to locate the exact position of the drain proved inconclusive due to a blockage. The client was informed of the possibility of the drain location within the footprint of the proposed extension, and the possible implications this would have if discovered at Stage 5. As the family was to continue living at the property for the duration of the contract period, the client instructed that the contract proceed at her own risk with the exact location of the drain to be determined at a later date, to minimise disruption in the initial stages.

Project issues

Insurances

RIBA Domestic Building Contract

The Contract sets out the liabilities of the parties, but allows them to decide the types and levels of insurance required.

In clause 6, it states that the contractor's liabilities include:

Loss or damage to the Works
Loss of or damage to products or equipment's
Death or bodily harm to any person working for the Contractor in connection with the Works
Loss or damage to property caused by contractor's negligence in carrying out the works. Death or bodily harm to a third person (not an employee of the contractor) caused by the Works.
On the hand the customer's liabilities are listed as including:
Loss or damage to existing structures and fixtures (if applicable)
Damage to neighboring property caused by the nature of the Works and not due to the Contractor's negligence in carrying out the Works.

The contract provides that the parties are free to specify the insurance policies required for the project as well as which of the parties (the customer or the contractor) would have responsibility to maintain each policy. The parties are also expected to specify the level of insurance (amount) and the period the insurance should be maintained for in the Contract Details. All insurance taken out by the Contractor is to be in the joint name of parties.

The guidance notes to the contract suggest that for the Contractor such insurance policies may include:

all risks insurance to cover its liability's for damages to the works, products or equipment,
public liability insurance to cover its liability for damages to third parties and property
any other insurance that the Customer may specifically request
For the customer, the guidance notes suggest the following options:
insurance for existing structures and fixtures,
insurance for damage to neighboring properties caused by the works and not the negligence of the contractor
comprehensive insurance covering all project risks.

If the contractor design option (optional clause A2) is selected, clause A2.7 requires that contractor should ensure that adequate professional indemnity insurance is maintained to cover its design responsibility; this would be specified in item L of the Contract Details.

The contract also provides an option for the customer to require that the contractor take out an insurance backed guarantee, this protects the customer if the contractor ceases to trade, and may also cover the costs of replacing defective materials and putting right poor workmanship. Some trade associations provide such guarantees on behalf of their members and it is a cost effective way of dealing with the risk of insolvencies in this segment of the market.

RIBA Concise Building Contract

The insurance provisions in both RIBA forms are broadly similar. Like the domestic version, the concise contract sets out the liabilities of the parties, but allows them to decide the types and levels of insurance required.

In clause 6, it states that the contractor's liabilities include:

Loss or damage to the Works
Loss of or damage to products or equipment's
Death or bodily harm to any person working for the Contractor in connection with the Works
Loss or damage to property caused by contractor's negligence in carrying out the works.
Death or bodily harm to a third person (not an employee of the contractor) caused by the Works.
On the hand the Employer's liabilities are listed as including:
Loss or damage to existing structures and fixtures
Damage to neighboring property caused by the nature of the Works and not due to the Contractor's negligence in carrying out the Works.

The contract also provides that the parties are free to specify the insurance policies required for the project as well as which of the parties (the Employer or the contractor) would have responsibility to maintain each policy. The parties should also specify the level of insurance (amount) and the period the insurance should be maintained for. All insurance taken out by the Contractor is to be in the joint name of parties.

The guidance notes to the contract suggest that for the Contractor such insurance policies may include:

all risks insurance to cover its liability's for damages to the works, products or equipment,

public liability insurance to cover its liability for damages to third parties and property

any other insurance that the Customer may specifically request

For the Employer, the guidance notes suggest the following options:

insurance for existing structures and fixtures,

insurance for damage to neighboring properties caused by the works and not the negligence of the contractor

comprehensive insurance covering all project risks.

If the contractor design option (optional clause A2) is selected, clause A2.7 requires that contractor ensures that adequate professional indemnity insurance is maintained.

JCT Intermediate Building Contract (IC11) and JCT Intermediate Building Contract with contractor's design (ICD11)

The contractor indemnifies the employer for injury to persons (for employees by an employer's liability policy and for third parties by a public liability policy) and damage to neighbouring property (also by a public liability policy) and must provide insurance for this. The minimum cover is £250,000 but insurers recommend £2,000,000 for any one occurrence. The liability is however unlimited in common law. The contractor is not liable for injury caused through an act of the employer, or a person for whom the employer is responsible. For damage to property the contractor is only liable due to his own negligence or breach of statutory duty.

Damage to adjoining buildings where there has been no negligence by the contractor (ie where the contractor has taken reasonable care) is not covered but a special policy can be taken out for the benefit of the employer. The amount of cover must be entered in the contract particulars and the contact administrator must instruct the contractor to take out this insurance. The cost is added to the contract sum and the policy taken out in joint names and placed with insurers approved by the employer. This can be expensive but must be in place from the start of work on site.

There are three alternative provisions for insurance of the works:

Option A – insurance taken out by the contractor.

Option B – insurance taken out by the employer.

Option C – applicable where work is being carried out to existing buildings which includes two insurances, both taken out by the employer. The existing structure and contents must be insured against 'Specified Perils' as defined in clause 6.8 and new works in or extensions to existing buildings must be covered by an 'All Risks' insurance policy.

There are also optional provisions requiring the contractor to take out insurance for non-negligent damage to property other than the works under clause 6.5.

The contractor must provide evidence of the insurance taken out and if this is not provided the employer can take out insurance and deduct the cost from the contract sum.

Compliance with the Joint Fire Code, to be complied with by both contractor and employer, may reduce the cost of some insurance policies.

Where ICD11 (with Contractor's Design) is being used the contractor is required to carry PI cover. The level and amount must be inserted in the contract particulars and the contractor must provide evidence of cover.

The contract administrator must explain the provisions of the contract to the employer and monitor the activities involved. The employer should be advised to take advice from their own insurance experts concerning suitability of wording and policies. The contract administrator should review the wording for unnecessary exceptions or restrictions but responsibility will rest with the employer and their insurance advisers.

For further information refer to Guide to the *JCT Intermediate Building Contract IC11* by Sarah Lupton (2011).

JCT Minor Works Building Contract (MW11) and JCT Minor Works Building Contract with contractor's design (WWD11)

As with IC11 the contractor indemnifies the employer for injury to persons and damage to neighbouring property caused by negligence and must demonstrate insurance for this. There are three options for insurance of the works:

Option A – insurance taken out by the contractor (for new buildings).

Option B – insurance taken out by the employer (for existing buildings and associated new works).

Option C – applicable where work is being carried out to existing buildings which includes two insurances, one taken out by the employer for the existing building and the other by the contractor for the works.

There is no provision for the Joint Fire Code. There is also no provision for insurance against damage to property which is not the result of negligence by the contractor. It may be appropriate to take out a special policy to cover this.

For further information refer to *Guide to the JCT Minor Works Building Contract MW11* by Sarah Lupton (2011).

JCT Building Contract for a Home Owner/Occupier (HO/B and HO/C)

Under the JCT Homeowner contract (both with and without a consultant to oversee the work), the 'customer' must tell their household insurers about the work taking place. The contractor must have an 'all risks' insurance policy to cover himself/herself and the customer for the full costs of damage to the works and to unfixed materials which are on the premises before being used in the work. The contractor must also have an up-to-date public liability policy for death or injury to people and damage to property. The amount of insurance is to be noted in the contract to cover any one claim arising from one event.

Contract administrator's powers and duties

RIBA Domestic Building Contract

Under the RIBA Domestic Building Contract 2014, the contract administrator has the following powers:

Clause	
3.2.2	Hold a meeting to resolve an event that may affect the progress of the works or contract price
3.3.2	When determining an application for a Revision of Time or additional payment, take into account the failure of the contractor to comply with 3.2.1(provide advance warning of an event that may affect progress of the works or contract price) and/or 3.3.1 (take reasonable steps to minimise the effect of the event in 3.2.1)
5.1	Administer the contract, send out instructions, issue certificates and take decision.
5.3	Visit the site and off site locations in connection with the works, inspect the works and reject defective work.
5.4	Issue instructions (change to work instructions, instructions on tests and inspections, instructions rejecting works, instructions postponing works among others)
5.5	Power to instruct that covered work be uncovered and inspected/ tested.
5.5.3	Power to accept work not in accordance with the contract and adjust the contract price accordingly.
5.7.4	Power to instruct that oral instructions do not take effect until confirmed by the contract administrator.
5.10.2	Power to determine the appropriate Revision of time and/or additional payment necessary as a result of a change to works instruction
5.11	Instruction resolving inconsistency in the Contract Documents and/or an instruction, or between the Contract Document and / or instruction with the law.

7.1 and 7.5	Issue a payment certificate as required under the contract. Or issue a payment certificate within 10 days of an application by the contractor (even if the amount is zero or negative)
7.8.3	Issue a final Payment Certificate
9.11.2	Make a fair decision on the appropriate revision of time and amend the Date for Completion accordingly.
9.14	Make a fair decision on an application for additional payment
9.16.1	Issue a Certificate of Practical Completion
10.3.4	Issue a notice to the Contractor to fix defects identified during the Defects Fixing Period.
12.3	Issue notice of intention to terminate
12.10	Certify final payment in the event of termination
A2.2	Comment on Contractor design proposal
A4.1	Issue payment certificates when a milestone has been achieved.
A5.1.4	Issue appropriate instructions in the event of the termination of the appointment of a Required Specialists.

Under the RIBA Domestic Building Contract 2014, the contract administrator has the following duties:

Clause	
3.4.1	If requested, advice the Customer on the contractor's proposal for improvement and cost savings.
5.2	Give the contractor, 2 free copies of the Contract Documents and send any updates promptly.
5.8	Advice the Customer to employ other contractors to carry out instructions that the Contractor has failed to carry out after notice.
5.10	Aim to agree with the Contractor on an application for Revision of Time or additional payment as a result of a change to works order.
6.4	Receive at the start of the project evidence of insurance policies and request evidence of up-to-date policy from time to time.
7.8.1	Aim to agree with the contractor on the final Contract Price

9.11	Aim to agree with the contractor on an application for a Revision of Time
9.14	Aim to agree with the contractor on an application for additional payment
9.16.2	Inform the contractor on why it disagrees that Practical Completion has been achieved.
9.18	Issue a notice identifying the areas to be taken over by the customer before practical completion is certified.
10.1	Advice the Customer to deduct liquidated damages
10.3.3	Notify the parties that all defects identified during the Defects Fixing Period have been fixed.
11.11	Confirm the agreed communication procedure (including electronic communication) or issue instructions on required. communication procedure
A8.1	Keep and update the Risks Register

RIBA Concise Building Contract

Under the RIBA Concise Building Contract 2014, the contract administrator has the following powers:

Clause	
3.2.2	Hold a meeting to resolve an event that may affect the progress of the works or contract price
3.3.2	When determining an application for a Revision of Time or additional payment, take into account the failure of the contractor to comply with 3.2.1(provide advance warning of an event that may affect progress of the works or contract price) and/or 3.3.1 (take reasonable steps to minimise the effect of the event in 3.2.1)
3.6	Attend progress meetings and invite other persons required to attend
5.1	Administer the contract, send out instructions, issue certificates and take decision.
5.3	Visit the site and off site locations in connection with the works, inspect the works and reject defective work.

5.4	Issue instructions (change to work instructions, instructions on tests and inspections, instructions rejecting works, instructions postponing works among others)
5.6.4	Power to instruct that oral instructions do not take effect until confirmed by the contract administrator.
5.7	Power to instruct that covered work be uncovered and inspected/tested.
5.8	Power to accept work not in accordance with the contract and adjust the contract price accordingly.
5.10	Modify, amend or confirm an instruction after the contractor has notified it has issues with the instruction.
5.13.2	Determine the appropriate Revision of time and/or additional payment necessary as a result of a change to works instruction
5.14	Instructions resolving inconsistency in the Contract Documents and/or an instruction, or between the Contract Document and / or instruction with the law.
9.11.2	Make a fair decision on the appropriate revision of time and amend the Date for Completion accordingly.
9.14	Make a fair decision on an application for additional payment
9.16.1	Issue a Certificate of Practical Completion
10.3.2	Issue a notice to the Contractor to fix defects identified during the Defects Fixing Period.
12.1	Issue notice of intention to terminate
12.8	Certify final payment in the event of termination
A2.2	Comment on Contractor design proposal
A4.1	Issue payment certificates when the works has reached practical completion.
A4.3	Issue payment certificates on the anticipated dates for achieving a milestone set out by the parties.
A7.1.4	Issue appropriate instructions in the event of the termination of the appointment of a Required Specialists.

Under the RIBA Concise Building Contract 2014, the contract administrator has the following duties:

Clause	
3.4.1	If requested, advice the Customer on the contractor's proposal for improvement and cost savings.
5.2	Give the contractor, 2 free copies of the Contract Documents and send any updates promptly.
5.11	Advice the Customer to employ other contractors to carry out instructions that the Contractor has failed to carry out after notice.
5.13	Aim to agree with the Contractor on an application for Revision of Time or additional payment as a result of a change to works order.
6.4	Receive at the start of the project evidence of insurance policies and request evidence of up-to-date policy from time to time.
7.3	No later than 5 days after the due date for interim payment, issue an interim payment certificate(even if the amount is zero or negative)
7.11.2	Aim to agree with the contractor on the final Contract Price
7.13	Not later than 5 days after the final payment Due Date, issue a final Payment Certificate.
9.14	Aim to agree with the contractor on an application for additional payment
9.16.2	Inform the contractor on why it disagrees that Practical Completion has been achieved.
9.18.1	Issue a notice identifying the areas to be taken over by the customer before practical completion is certified.
10.1	Advice the Customer to deduct liquidated damages
10.3.1	Notify the parties that all defects identified during the Defects Fixing Period have been fixed.

11.11	Confirm the agreed communication procedure (including electronic communication) or issue instructions on required communication procedure.
A10.1	Keep and update the Risks Register

JCT Intermediate Building Contract (IC11)
JCT Intermediate Building Contract with contractor's design (ICD11)

Under IC11 the contract administrator has the following powers:

Clause	
2.9	Instruct errors in setting out can remain.
2.17	Consent to removal of goods from site.
2.30	Instruct defects are not to be made good.
3.5	Consent to domestic subcontractors.
3.11.1	Issue instructions requiring a variation.
3.11.1/3.11.4	Sanction a variation by the contractor.
3.12	Issue instructions postponing work.
3.14/3.15	Require contractor to open up work/get work tested.
3.16.1	Issue instructions requiring removal of work not in accordance with the contract.
3.16.2	Issue instructions regarding work not carried out in a proper and workmanlike manner.
3.17	Exclude persons from the site.
6.5.1	Instruct 6.5.1 insurance is taken out.
8.4.1	Give contractor notice of default(s).
Schedule 2	Issue instructions naming a person as subcontractor.

Under IC11 the contract administrator has the following duties:

Clause	
1.9	Send copies of certificates to the employer and contractor at the same time.
2.8.2.1	Provide contractor with copies of contract documents.
2.8.2.2	Provide contractor with further copies of contract drawings and specification/schedules of work/contract bills.
2.9	Determine any levels that may be required.
2.10	Provide contractor with copies of information referred to in the information release schedule.
2.11	Provide contractor with such further drawings as are reasonably necessary and issue necessary instructions.
2.13	Issue instructions regarding errors, inconsistencies or divergences in contract documents.
2.15.1	Issue instructions regarding any discrepancies/divergences discovered between contract documents and statutory requirements.
2.19.1	Give extension of time (if contractor submits a notice and contract administrator considers completion date will be delayed and delay caused by a relevant event).
2.21	Certify Practical Completion.
2.22	Issue certificate(s) of non-completion.
2.25	Issue statement regarding partial possession.
2.30	Notify contractor of defects.
2.31	Issue certificate of making good.
3.7/Schedule 2	Issue instructions with regard to named subcontractors.
3.10	Comply with contractor's request for empowering provision.
3.13	Issue instructions regarding provisional sums.

4.7	Certify interim payments.
4.7.1.2	Certify interim payment on Practical Completion.
4.14	Issue final certificate.
4.17	Ascertain or instruct quantity surveyor to ascertain any amounts of direct loss and/or expense incurred.
6.5.1	Where required, instruct contractor to take out joint names insurance policy.

JCT Minor Works Building Contract (MW11)
JCT Minor Works Building Contract with contractor's design (MWD11)

Under MW11 the contract administrator has the following powers:

Clause	
2.5.2	Express satisfaction with Contractor's Proposal to deal with inconsistency in CDP documents.
2.10/2.11	Instruct that defects can remain.
3.3.1	Consent to domestic subcontractors.
3.4	Issue written instructions to the contractor.
3.6.1	Issue variations, including additions to or omissions from the works and the order or period in which they are to be carried out.
3.6.2	Agree the price of variations with the contractor before they are carried out.
3.8	Exclude employed persons from the site.
4.5.5	Issue 'pay less notice' on behalf of employer.
6.4.1	Give the contractor notice of defaults.

Under MW11 the contract administrator has the following duties:

Clause	
2.3/2.4	Issue any further information necessary.
2.3/2.4	Issue all certificates.
2.4/2.5.1	Correct inconsistencies between contract documents.
2.7/2.8	Make such extensions of time as may be reasonable.
2.9/2.10	Certify Practical Completion.
2.10/2.11	Certify that defects have been made good.
3.4/3.4.1	Confirm instructions in writing.
3.6.2	Endeavour to agree value of variation with contractor.
3.6.3	Value variation instructions.
3.6.3	Ascertain amount of direct loss and/or expense.
3.7	Issue instructions regarding expenditure of provisional sums.
4.3	Issue interim certificates.
4.4	Certify payment after Practical Completion.
4.8.1	Issue final certificate.
5.4A.3	Issue certificates regarding insurance monies to be paid to the contractor.
5.4B.2	Issue instructions regarding reinstatement and making good of loss or damage.

For advice on completing the contract and associated administration forms refer to the IC11 and MW11 Project Packs available from www.ribabookshops.com. These include notes on completing the recitals, articles and particulars in the contract as well as the standard forms: architect's/contract administrator's instruction, notification of extension of time, certificate of progress payment, non-completion certificate, Practical Completion certificate, certificate of making good and final certificate. They also contain useful checklists.

JCT Building Contract for a Home Owner/Occupier (HO/B and HO/C)

Under HO/C the 'consultant' has the following duties:

Clause
Inspect the building work to see whether the contractor is generally keeping to his responsibilities under the Building Contract.
Advise about how any changes to the building work will affect the planned timescales and costs.
Give instructions to the contractor and extend deadlines if necessary while the building work is being done.
Check the builder's invoices and make sure they are accurate and if necessary explain the invoice to the customer.
When the building work or each stage of the work is finished to his/her reasonable satisfaction, issue a certificate to both the customer and the contractor which shows the finish date.
Give the contractor a list of any faults which have appeared at any time up to three months after the finish date and which the contractor must put right.
When the contractor has put right all the faults listed by the 'consultant', issue a certificate to the customer and the contractor to confirm this.
Any other services as written into the contract.

Architect:
MVRDV and Mole
Architects

Date completed:
August 2009

Construction cost:
Confidential

MVRDV were approached to design the first of a series of holiday homes in the countryside. The brief was that the house should be equally suitable for two or eight inhabitants.

The Balancing Barn provides a changing relationship to the nature outside, experienced first at ground level and then mid-air at tree-top level. The structure balances on a central concrete core, with the section that sits on the ground constructed from heavier materials than the cantilevered section. The long sides of the structure are well concealed by trees, offering privacy inside and around the barn.

Constructional challenges included the coordination of the steel 'bridge' structure with the prefabricated timber insulated panels, and dealing with both the live movement and permanent deflection of the steel. The house has a 'handmade' quality, the result of detailed design in collaboration with manufacturers' technical departments as well as operatives on site.

Mole Architects partnered MVRDV and were responsible for planning drawings and producing working drawings for construction. Both architects were separately employed by the client through all stages of the contract, with the architects working in partnership to deliver the project. Fee structures reflected the changing roles of the two architects, with MVRDV starting with a higher proportion of the fee during design stages, reducing as Mole ran the job on site; during Stage 4 the fee split was equal.

The house was procured by competitive tender and let on a traditional JCT Intermediate Contract with Quantities; a cost consultant was retained during the contract period and administered the contract. Mole worked closely with many domestic subcontractors during the build to refine details; additional design work was carried out on the sliding windows, stainless steel cladding, structural steelwork and M&E design and internal joinery during the contract period.

Practice issues

Professional indemnity insurance

All practices must carry at least £250,000 of professional indemnity (PI) insurance, which can be obtained through the RIBA Insurance Agency (go to www.architectspi. com), currently costing from around £450pa. However, whilst necessary, PI is a last resort and it is important to manage risks, especially those related to projects.

Dealing with a claim from a client for breach of professional duty is extremely time-consuming and can be depressing and morale-sapping. It is important to establish procedures to identify and manage risks so that claims are, at worst, infrequent, and preferably non-existent.

Sources of information on identifying and managing risk

There are several sources of sound advice on identifying and managing risk, including the RIBA *Good Practice Guide: Keeping out of Trouble*. PI insurers can often provide good risk management advice: for example, the RIBA Insurance Agency undertakes regular risk management audits of member practices to help improve processes and thus minimise the risk of a claim.

The RIBA, in association with the RIBA Insurance Agency, has produced a short guide entitled *Understanding Risk Management*, which has been designed to assist architects in understanding and managing risk within their business. (This can be downloaded from www.architectsPI.com/pages/ riskmanagement.aspx.)

The potential risks to the practice should be considered and assessed according to the likelihood of them occurring and the severity of the impact should they do so. A simple matrix can be developed to show these two variables, which will show clearly the most significant potential issues. Risk management plans should be reviewed regularly (at least annually) and updated as necessary.

Refer also to Stage 2: Risk management.

> ## Stage summary

The extent of the architect's duties during Stage 5 will depend largely on the form of contract, and whether or not the role of contract administrator is part of the remit. For small projects it is likely that it will be, although some domestic clients will look to deal directly with the contractor to save the cost of fees. Explain to the client the important issues that will need to be addressed and the need to make sure they have a proper contract in place. (In that instance the JCT HO/B would be the most appropriate.) The new RIBA Domestic and Concise building contracts will fill many gaps that exist within the suite of documents currently available and have the potential to be transformative for small projects, giving the ability to use contractor and sub-contractor design on domestic projects, amongst a number of other features.

If you are not involved in Stage 5 activities it is unlikely you will be involved in Stage 6 but remember to keep in touch with the client periodically and show an interest in how the project proceeds. When it is complete you may want to take photographs for your records and for marketing/business development purposes (make sure you get permission for this). You will then be in a good position to help out should any be needed or to pick up further work at a later stage.

If you have been involved in the construction stage, Stage 6 is an opportunity to see how the building is performing as well as making sure it is properly completed by the contractor and the post-completion administration properly executed.

Stage 6

Handover & Close Out

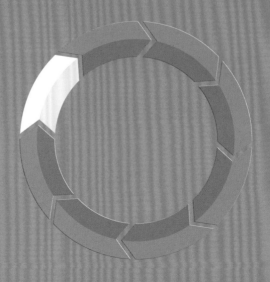

RIBA Plan of Work 2013 Stage 6

RIBA
Plan of
Work
2013

Stage 6

Handover and Close Out

Task Bar	Tasks
Core Objectives	Handover of building and conclusion of **Building Contract**.
Procurement Variable task bar	Conclude administration of **Building Contract**.
Programme Variable task bar	*There are no specific activities in the RIBA Plan of Work 2013.*
(Town) Planning Variable task bar	*There are no specific activities in the RIBA Plan of Work 2013.*
Suggested Key Support Tasks	Carry out activities listed in **Handover Strategy** including **Feedback** for use during the future life of the building or on future projects. Updating of **Project Information** as required. *The priority during this stage is the successful handover of the building and concluding the **Building Contract** with support tasks focused on evaluating performance and providing **Feedback** for use on future projects. Fine tuning of the building services is likely to occur.*
Sustainability Checkpoints	• *Has assistance with the collation of post-completion information for final sustainability certification been provided?*
Information Exchanges (at stage completion)	Updated **'As-constructed' Information**.
UK Government Information Exchanges	Required.

Introduction

Stage 6 maps broadly to the former Stage L.

The stage involves three groups of activities:

— The Defects Liability Period (DLP).
— Soft Landings.
— Post-occupancy Evaluation (POE).

The extent and nature of the activities undertaken during Stage 6 will very much depend upon what you have been contracted to do under the client appointment. There is enormous potential benefit and value to clients in the activities Stage 6 brings but for some the cost will be perceived as being too great, particularly if the budget has been stretched during the construction activities in Stage 5. A well-managed project will have made allowance for Stage 6 activities at the outset however and must be properly considered during Stage 0. For small projects the level of input can be trimmed to suit any financial constraints but some allowance should be made.

DLP activities will be more straightforward if construction has been managed and monitored regularly. In theory there should be no 'snags' at Practical Completion. This is difficult to achieve in practice but should be the aim and this should be made clear to the contractor in the tender documents and as work on site progresses.

Despite this, there are likely to be some defects at the conclusion of the 6- or 12-month DLP and these must be dealt in accordance with the contract conditions.

'Soft Landings' is a process that commences at the start of the commission and as such these activities are noted at the relevant stage in the book. Where the activities take place after PC they are noted in this section. They will only be relevant if they have been commissioned at the outset and included in the appointment. They can be added as a variation during the course of the project but will have less effect and some catching up may be required.

POE can be:

— In-house, primarily for the benefit of the designer, including a debriefing for those involved.
— A full post-project evaluation, involving monitoring of the building's performance. It is usual for such work to be commissioned separately from the original appointment. Such exercises are generally considered to be of greater use to clients and project teams with multiple Project Programmes.

Stage 6, like Stage 7, can be an opportunity:

— To keep in touch with the client and/or building user with a view to future commissions (on that building or other ones).
— To get recommendations to other clients.

 According to RIBA Business Benchmarking data, between one-third and three-fifths of most practices' workload derives from repeat business, so this is an important area to focus on.

Project activities

Information required

DLP activities

| 1. | Copies of the construction phase plan developed by the contractor. |

| 2. | Sets of administration forms appropriate for the form of contract being used. |

| 3. | Energy performance certificate. |

Soft Landings activities

Note: the brief for Soft Landings and POE activities must be agreed at an early stage in the project, ideally at Stage 1.

| 1. | As-installed information for services, construction detailing, etc (if responsible for producing the energy performance certificate). |

It is important to ensure that health and safety file information is collected and provided to the principal designer and not lost within any other as-installed information.

| 2. | Brief from the occupier on their operational requirements. |

| 3. | Part L log book. |

POE activities

| 1. | Energy use data, eg utility bills. |

Stage activities

DLP activities

1.	Conclude administration of the Building Contract, including the 3-, 6- or 12-month defects inspection as applicable.
2.	There will be a prescribed programme for DLP activities after Practical Completion, usually for 6 or 12 months. A programme for activities for Soft Landings and POE will need to be agreed with the client during an earlier stage, ideally in Stage 1.
3.	On practical Completion remind the client that responsibility for insurance reverts to them.
4.	Conduct in-house appraisal of office performance on the project.
5.	Consider holding a debriefing exercise with the client and other consultants.
6.	Check if the building log book for the building operator – required by Part L of the Building Regulations – has been issued. The building log book should be in accordance with the requirements of CIBSE TM31 (refer to www.cibse.org).
7.	Participate in the creation of operating manuals for the building. See BSRIA BG 1/2007TK for recommended contents of these manuals (refer to www.bsria.co.uk).

Soft Landings activities

1.	If accredited for energy performance certificate (EPC) administration, check if the client wants to instruct this and, if so, agree fees.

EPCs are required for all buildings when they are constructed, leased or sold. In newly constructed or refurbished buildings the EPC will normally be provided by the main contractor.

For information on EPCs refer to the UK government website at www.gov.uk and search for 'energy performance certificates'.

For clarification on exceptions for providing EPCs and what they should cover, refer to the relevant guide at www.communities.gov.uk.

2.	Check if the client wants to instruct the design team to undertake continuous commissioning, 'sea trials' and Soft Landings, etc. If so, agree a scope of service for the additional service and fee. Agreement for this service should be confirmed prior to going to tender.

A Soft Landings team (designer and constructor) is resident on site during the move-in period to ensure that emerging issues are dealt with effectively. The team can then monitor building use and energy performance for the first two or three years of occupation, identifying opportunities both for fine tuning the building and for improvements in future developments. The process also creates a coordinated route to POE. Sea trials are where the design team is involved in running the building for the first two years.

3.	If a BREEAM assessment has been commissioned you may need to provide information to the BREEAM assessor in order for the post-occupancy stage of the assessment to be completed.

A full BREEAM assessment is undertaken in four to five stages (depending on when the assessor is appointed), comprising: registration, pre-assessment, initial guidance/design stage assessment, construction and post-construction review/final certification.

A BREEAM certificate will not be issued until after the post-construction stage of the assessment has been completed. For further guidance refer to www.breeam.org.

4.	If appointed as information manager, assist in the Soft Landings processes and coordinate and release the 'end of construction' BIM record model data. Review the Project Performance In Use and compare with projected BIM data. Invite and coordinate Feedback from all stakeholders in the process and disseminate to all in order to benefit future projects.

5.	Check whether the client has issued an instruction for an energy performance certificate prior to selling or leasing the building.
6.	For residential schemes where the Code for Sustainable Homes (CSH) is required, complete the post-construction review of the CSH assessment so that 'final' code certification can be issued.
7.	For non-domestic buildings, undertake the post-completion stage of the BREEAM assessment if required.
8.	Provide a copy of a building user guide if required. *The guide will contain the information that will be relevant to the non-technical building user to explain how the building systems operate to increase comfort levels, etc. This might include an on-site presentation.*
9.	Ensure that seasonal commissioning is undertaken, so that HVAC systems are commissioned for both summer and winter conditions, as agreed with the client.
10.	Debriefing and Feedback are management exercises. If it is agreed to extend the commission to include these, establish the scope and content of Soft Landings and POE activities. Do not allow an exercise to be undertaken if it seems likely that it might result in recriminations – and even arbitration or litigation. Always inform your PI insurers before embarking on any Feedback study.
11.	Check whether the design and technical teams would cooperate in debriefing.
12.	Check whether the client would cooperate in debriefing. In-house appraisal is a healthy operation for nearly all projects, but participants must feel able to exchange views freely. Debriefing can become a sensitive matter and will only succeed with the full cooperation of all involved.
13.	Raise with all consultants the desirability of engaging in a systematic analysis of the management, construction and performance of the project.

14.	Arrange a series of debriefing meetings.
	Convene debriefing meetings upon completion to evaluate technical matters.
	Involve all design team members, the main contractor and possibly the client. At debriefing meetings, watch out for partisan or defensive attitudes. Honest and objective discussion should not be allowed to degenerate into acrimony.
	Record the discussions and formulate overall conclusions from the debriefing.
15.	Make visits to the site to make structured transfer of information to the users and the facilities management team.
16.	Spot emerging issues and solve problems arising.
17.	Establish a method of providing ongoing assistance to the users.

POE activities

1.	Check to see if the client wishes to undertake a BREEAM In-Use Assessment of the building in operation and agree the scope of the service and the fee.
	BREEAM In-Use is a scheme to help building managers reduce the running costs and improve the environmental performance of buildings.
2.	Check if the client wants to instruct a POE exercise and, if so, agree the scope of service and the fee.
3.	Advise the client of the need to employ other consultants and the contractor.
4.	If a full Feedback study is planned, agree with the client what access will be available, what the timescale should be and in what form the findings should be presented.

5.	If the building is occupied by a public authority or an institution providing a public service to a large number of persons, with a total useful area greater than 1000m^2, check if the client has issued an instruction for a display energy certificate.
6.	Explain to the client the purpose of a debriefing exercise or full post-project evaluation and that their Feedback might be a key part of this activity. Discuss to what extent key persons in the organisation could be expected to contribute opinions at a meeting chaired by the architect (see BRE Digest 478 for guidance).
7.	Arrange a meeting with key personnel from the client organisation (the building users and maintenance staff). Ensure that you have considered your objectives and what information you want to get from this exercise, and have a clear agenda for the meeting.
8.	Discuss with the client to what extent the managers and users of the project could be expected to cooperate in completing a questionnaire.
9.	Discuss with the client whether authorised photographers would be allowed access after final completion, for Feedback purposes.
10.	Discuss with the client whether it would be permissible for the architect to carry out a survey of the building In Use sometime after completion.
11.	Check with your PI insurers that you have cover for Feedback activities.
12.	Consider the desirability of a full Feedback study or a post-project evaluation.
13.	Year 1: — Recalculate capital and revenue target costs at current rates. — Identify the actual capital costs. Year 2 (and 3): — Identify/provide data required for the review. — Agree a programme of meetings.

— Identify the issues, establish causes and consider remedies.
— Contribute to the output reports and recommendations.
— If instructed, implement the recommendations.

| 14. | Participate in the BREEAM In-Use Assessment process if required. |

| 15. | Seek approvals as required by the building occupier to undertake post-occupancy tests. |

| 16. | Keep records of time costs for POE activities. |

Information exchange

| 1. | 'As-constructed' Information updated in response to ongoing client Feedback and maintenance or operational developments. |

DLP activities

| 1. | Certificate of making good defects. |

This is issued when defects listed at the end of the defects liability period have been remedied.

| 2. | Final certificate. |

The issue of the final certificate brings the authority of the contract administrator, under the terms of the Building Contract, to a close. The contractor's liability continues until the end of the limitation period. There might, in addition or alternatively, be contract provisions which refer to statements issued by the contract administrator or by the employer (eg in the case of design and build contracts). These should be regarded as requiring the same care and consideration as certificates before being issued. Case law has confirmed that there is no immunity from negligence in certifying.

3.	Updating facilities management BIM model data, as asset changes are made.
4.	Study of parametric object information contained within BIM model data.

Soft Landings activities

1.	Energy performance certificate.
2.	Operating manual/building user guide, if part of scope.
3.	Records of trials and their recommendations.

POE activities

1.	Record of conclusions reached at debriefing meetings, distributed to participants.
2.	Results of full Feedback study conducted with the client or user client, or everyday users of the building, perhaps several years post completion. It is essential that the benefits and lessons learned from appraisals are passed to all members of staff. The office quality plan, manuals and procedures might need amendment or revision as a result.

Sustainability Checkpoint 6

Sustainability aims

To support the client in the early stages of occupation and to provide aftercare services as agreed.

Key actions

1.	Assist with collation of post-completion information for final sustainability certification.
2.	Observe building operation In Use and assist with fine tuning and guidance for occupants.
3.	Issue declaration of energy/carbon performance In Use (eg Carbon Buzz).
4.	If necessary, review the project sustainability features and operation methods with the client, facilities managers and occupants.
5.	Assist with the fine tuning of building services and operational systems to check that they meet user requirements.

This project consisted of a replacement barn built on the grounds of the architect's farmstead. Initially proposed as a functional creative space for varying uses, it has been a temporary office and is now a temporary home whilst the rest of the farm is redeveloped. Its modular frame allows for easy adaptation and future flexibility, being built at a scale that is both agricultural and domestic.

This was a self-build project, so we needed a form of construction that was easy to erect and clad, without being dependent on heavy plant and machinery. The parallam frame was templated and machined by the local carpenter and the timber frame panels made down the hill at the local timber frame company.

The living and dining area are in one half of the barn structure, and the bedrooms and children's play area in the other. The bathroom, kitchen and services are located in the middle, in the same structural bay as the entrance.

The material palette is one of practical economy; stained timber cladding and corrugated sheet to the exterior; concrete floor, dry lining boards to the walls, plywood to the ceiling internally. Rather than plaster over the dry lining boards, as designed, a fermacell board (sometimes used in art galleries) was selected and a feature made of the expressed edges to form a tile effect to the walls. The internal partition walls that separate the play area from the bedrooms are built from birch-faced plywood pinned to a softwood frame. All timber surfaces were limed to provide uniformity.

Heating is provided by two Dutch tile stoves, one in each main space. This is the primary source of heat to the temporary home, and during the heating season they are only lit twice a day to provide enough heat. All other services are contained within the service zone of kitchen, bathroom and loft space for water tank and flues, with power in exposed conduit ducting. This provides future flexibility for rewiring to different layouts and uses.

> Project issues

Monitoring building performance/POE

POE is a separate activity and will only occur where the appointment includes it (see also 'Soft Landings' below) and this is frequently not the case with small projects.

That aside, the investigations for Feedback, which might not be practicable until a year or more after completion of the project, could include structured interviews with the building users, access to the buildings, and access to information and records held by various team members. None of these activities should be attempted if there is a risk of inviting acrimony and dispute, although there is significant potential value in terms of continued client relations, learning from Feedback and aiding continuous improvement.

The purpose of a post-project evaluation is to analyse the management, construction and performance of a project and could entail:

An analysis of the project records.

An inspection of the fabric of the completed building.

Studies of the building In Use.

Meetings and workshops with the client, consultants and users.

A post-project evaluation should cover:

The purpose of the study.

The description of the need.

Performance against cost, quality and timescale targets.

Client satisfaction with the project and the facility.

User satisfaction with the facility.

Performance and communication between project participants:

    Project sponsor.

    Client project manager.

    Where relevant, client advisor.

    Project team.

Overview and recommendations:

    Lessons learned.

    Major points of action.

    Costs.

Technical appendices:

    User survey data.

    Monitoring data.

Soft Landings

Soft Landings extends the duties of the team:

Before handover.

In the weeks immediately after handover.

For the first year of occupation.

For the second and third years.

It is critical that Soft Landings activities are commenced from the start of the project at Stage 1, not as an afterthought.

It comprises activities which improve the performance outcome of buildings. Designers and contractors remain involved with buildings after Practical Completion, helping fine tune the systems and ensuring that occupants understand how to operate their building.

The procedures are designed to augment standard professional scopes of service, not to replace them, and can be tailored to run alongside industry-standard Procurement routes. Soft Landings begins at the outset of the project, not just at handover. It includes better briefing, realistic performance benchmarking, reality-checking of design and Procurement decisions, a graduated handover process and a period of professional aftercare by the project team. Equally important, it promotes an open and collaborative working culture.

The main additions to normal scopes of service occur during five main stages:

1. Inception and briefing
To clarify the duties of members of the client, design and construction teams during critical stages, and to help set and manage expectations for performance In Use.

2. Design development and review (including specification and construction)
This proceeds much as usual, but with greater attention to applying the procedures established in the briefing stage, reviewing the likely performance against the original expectations and achieving specific outcomes.

3. Pre-handover

To take place with greater involvement of designers, builders, operators and commissioning and controls specialists, in order to strengthen the operational readiness of the building.

4. Initial aftercare

To take place during the users' settling-in period, with a resident representative or team on site to help pass on knowledge, respond to queries and react to problems.

5. Aftercare

In years 1 to 3 after handover, with periodic monitoring and review of building performance.

Core principles of Soft Landings

In order to provide greater clarity to the industry about the core fundamental requirements of a Soft Landings project, BSRIA has created a set of core principles:

1. Adopt the entire process

The project should be procured as a Soft Landings project, and project documentation should explicitly state that the project team will adopt the five work stages in the Soft Landings Framework to the extent possible.

2. Provide leadership

The client should show leadership, engender an atmosphere of trust and respect, support open and honest collaboration, and procure a design and construction process that can be conducted with equal levels of commitment from all disciplines.

3. Set roles and responsibilities

In Soft Landings, the client is an active participant, and leads the process at the outset to develop the roles and responsibilities. This should include client representatives, all key design professionals and the supply chain. The people involved in this process should be the actual individuals who will work on the project.

4. Ensure continuity

Soft Landings should be continuous throughout the contractual process. It should be made part of all later appointments, and expressed clearly in contracts and subcontract work packages as appropriate. The client and principal contractor should ensure that subcontractors and specialist contractors take their Soft Landings roles and responsibilities seriously.

5. Commit to aftercare

There should be a clear and expressed commitment by the client and project team to follow through with Soft Landings aftercare activities, and to observe, fine tune and review performance for three years post completion. The aftercare activities should aim to achieve the Soft Landings performance objectives, and any targets agreed at the design stage.

6. Share risk and responsibility

The client and principal contractor should create a culture of shared risk and responsibility. Incentives should be used to encourage the project team to deliver a high-performance building that matches the design intentions.

7. Use Feedback to inform design

The client's requirements, the design brief and the design response should be informed by performance Feedback from earlier projects. The desired operational outcomes need to be expressed clearly and realistically.

8. Focus on operational outcomes

The Soft Landings team should focus on the building's performance In Use. Regular reality-checking should be carried out to ensure that the detailed design and its execution continues to match the client's requirements, the design team's ambitions and any specific Project Objectives.

9. Involve the building managers

The organisation that will manage the finished building should have a meaningful input to the client's requirements and the formulation of the brief.

10. Involve the end users

Prospective occupants should be actively researched to understand their needs and expectations, which should inform the client's requirements and the design brief. There should be a clear process for managing expectations throughout the construction process and into building operation.

11. Set performance objectives

Performance objectives for the building should be set at the outset. They should be well-researched, appropriate and realistic, capable of being monitored and reality checked throughout design and construction, and measurable post completion in line with the client's key performance indicators.

12. Communicate and inform

Regardless of their legal and contractual obligations to one another, project team members need to be comfortable communicating with the entire team in order to achieve the levels of collaboration necessary to carry out Soft Landings activities.

Performance assessment and Feedback

Debriefing after completion is always a value-adding and worthwhile exercise, but it is often difficult to make the time for it with the pressures of managing the workload of current projects. It need not take up much time though, and filling out a standard form will help in this regard. You can adapt the contents to suit your particular needs, but headings might include:

Subject	Notes
Financial performance	
Office costs against planned expenditure (and therefore profit achieved)	
Project cost planning and final costs against budget	
Project issues	
Did the project meet/exceed the brief?	
Project quality control	
Meeting completion date	
Quality of building, both functionally and (as objectively as possible) aesthetically	
Project team	
Working relationship with client, design team members, principal designer, contractor	
Quality of work across the design team	
Quality of your own drawings, specifications, etc	
Success of Project Strategies (measured against the brief)	
Technology (ie IT and BIM)	
Communication	
Building Control	

317

Procurement	
Construction	
Handover	
Maintenance and Operation	
Sustainability	
Contractor's performance in terms of:	
Project management, quality of staff	
Site management, quality of staff	
Health and safety compliance	
Continuity of personnel	
Quality of work	
Effectiveness of programming	
Cooperation in settling claims	
Cooperation over material for the Health and Safety File	
Early identification of problems relating to progress, information and quality	
Disputes/potential disputes	
Financial arrangements, certificates, dayworks and measurement evaluation	

Prepare reports as appropriate, including a timetable for further reviews. Distribute the report and file as appropriate. Decide which drawings and documents should be kept. No office has the space to keep all project records indefinitely, but a set of project records, properly maintained and completed, should be a useful condensed history of the project – a point of reference for quick comparison of working methods, timescales and costs. Photographs of the Work in Progress and completed, presentation drawings and models should also be kept available for prospective clients and for general publicity purposes. However, it is essential to keep proper records of the kind of information that will be required in the event of disputes, in particular:

The client brief and related correspondence.

The contract documents.

Contract administrator's instructions.

Minutes of project meetings.

Certificates issued.

Notes of inspections and surveys.

Any crucial 'state of the art' information
(manufacturers' key information, current British Standards, codes, etc.)

Progress charts, etc.

Selected working drawings.

Risk Register for the project.

It is important to remember that the personnel involved with the project may not be available to give evidence if litigation occurs some years later.

Archiving

Archiving of material produced by the office needs to be managed and organised to allow easy retrieval, and forward thinking will save much time when a practice is asked to provide information to resolve a query about past work.

Decisions need to be made as to how archives are to be stored, how long they are to be kept and who has the authority to destroy records. Although contracts and PI insurances will differ, for many project documents there is a legal obligation to retain information relating to the contract, and it is in the interest of the office to retain drawings permanently as an archive of the work of the practice and as a design resource. The RIBA recommends that key project documents are retained for 17–20 years, because of the laws relating to the periods within which claims may be brought. In the event of a claim being made against the firm, or the firm wishing to make a claim, relevant documents will need to be readily accessible. This will be of utmost importance where, for example, a claim is made via the speedier dispute resolution procedures such as adjudication. Here the adjudicator will expect to see all relevant documentation to enable them to reach a decision within the 28-day period.

As noted above, the BIM protocols should highlight how electronic data will be recorded and stored throughout a project, and this data should be archived accordingly with the project documentation and data. Any information shared via a project website should be recorded, stored and archived locally as a record of information shared.

It would be good practice to record and appropriately archive other consultants' information and models issued to form part of a federated model at an agreed review stage. This information represents the level of coordination and completion of the design and contributes to the context of the architectural model.

All current records, information and other live data should be reviewed from time to time, at least annually, by senior staff. Files that are no longer current and regularly referenced should be archived. A register of archived files should be set up in each office to record all hard copy files archived. This should list details of each file (eg project number, file reference) and should also state the disposal date. The register of archived files should be reviewed annually by the person responsible for archiving who should, when disposal dates occur, ensure that the expired records are destroyed in a confidential manner. All archives, whether within the office or off-site, should be kept securely with access restricted to the person responsible for archives and persons specifically authorised by a senior member of staff.

If the project has been developed utilising a building information model to a sufficient level of definition then the model could be utilised by the client or building user to manage the facility. The final issue of the model should be recorded and archived accordingly, as the facilities management team may alter the model significantly to suit the management software. Archiving is the final process in the life of a job, and setting up filing and naming conventions correctly at the beginning of a project will ensure that the archiving process will be simpler to organise.

The storage of archived electronic data, and its security, should be considered as part of the general requirements of an IT section in the office or quality manual. Any policy for storing, archiving and where appropriate disposing of electronic data should follow that for hard copy documents.

Remodelling of the ground floor of 1970s buildings accommodating a Higher Education Research Centre.

Date completed:
November 2012

This project involved conversion of a loading bay and separate undersized entrances to two 1970s towers to create a single reception space with café and meeting facilities as well as new loading bay. The external public realm was also upgraded.

Construction cost:
£990,000

Contract:
GC Works Design and Build with novated design team

A 'more-for-less' approach was taken in designing the project, adding value to an existing building asset, and reducing energy use through improved fabric. Ensuring that every aspect of the design delivered maximum function and value was key to the success of the completed project. The design not only meets the functional requirements of the brief by providing a secure entrance, but also lifts the character of this part of the campus with a bold materials palette and design. What were simple lift lobbies have been redesigned so that they also function as social learning spaces and 'shop windows', allowing research departments in the buildings to display their work.

Awards:
Shortlisted for AJ Retrofit Award 2013

The project had to be constructed whilst the buildings and surrounding campus remained in operation. As the project involved the main entrances to the buildings it was important to design and plan phased construction work so it could be carried out whilst maintaining access and egress from the buildings, with fire escape being a particularly important aspect. There was very little area for site storage, welfare facilities or site offices.

A number of temporary access strategies were developed for inclusion in the tender documentation and tenderers were required to submit a construction logistics plan detailing their approach to the restricted site and their own phasing and access strategies. The successful contractor utilised a combination of swapping entrance routes to the site along with temporary plywood access 'tunnels' through the site which allowed work to continue in the majority of areas whilst safe access and fire escape were maintained for building users.

Practice issues

Becoming an RIBA Client Advisor

RIBA Client Advisors are architects who have been selected from the RIBA membership, having met a set of criteria that give them the skills to give advice on the composition and selection of the project team and provide independent advice to help the client run the project efficiently and achieve best value and quality. They are evaluated and accredited on an annual basis, and the RIBA maintains a register and provides shortlists of Client Advisors to potential clients. Client Advisors are independent from the project team.

Go to www.architecture.com for further advice and information on how to become a Client Advisor. To apply you will need to write a short personal statement. This will comprise a brief statement to demonstrate your knowledge, skills and experience in each of the five core competencies (vision and aspiration, stakeholder engagement, setting and safeguarding design quality, design value management and use) and your relevant project experience with three examples (maximum three images per project) and three references. (The RIBA will write to your referees.)

Benefits of becoming an RIBA Client Advisor

Provides an additional, alternative source of income.
An activity that can enhance your reputation and lead to further potential commissions for a standard architectural appointment.
Helps develop your knowledge of specialist project activities.

Benefits of becoming a chartered practice

Becoming a Chartered Practice is inexpensive (currently £110pa + VAT for sole practitioners and £140–180pa + VAT for practices of 2–10 people) and brings a number of benefits:

Promotion of your practice to potential clients by the RIBA.

Provides a mark of quality to clients.

Gives access to the annual business benchmarking survey.

To join you must meet a number of criteria, including having:

At least one director or partner who is an RIBA Chartered Member.

PI cover.

An operational QA system.

An appropriate health and safety policy.

An appropriate employment policy.

A written environmental policy

A CPD framework.

You must participate in the annual business benchmarking survey and you must also pay at least minimum wage to staff, including students.

For most practices these are things you already have in place, and if you don't, this book will help you get there! Go to www.architecture.com for further details.

Maximise your opportunities

To maximise your chances of winning work, make sure your practice details are kept up-to-date on www.architecture.com where you can upload projects and add, edit and delete information and images in your practice profile.

327

Keep records

Maintain records throughout the year of the benchmark data required for the annual survey to make the process more straightforward when you come to fill out the forms.

Stage summary

Stage 6 marks the end of the project, but the incorporation of the new Stage 7 is an encouragement to keep in touch, monitor the building's performance and maintain a relationship with the client, with a view to getting further commissions from them or referrals to other clients. The Plan of Work 2103 is cyclical: where one project finishes, the following ones can learn from it in a virtuous circle of continuous improvement. Most small projects will not provide the opportunity for fee income during Stage 7, but it is a reminder to do these things and in doing so to improve your offer and – with a fair wind – increase turnover and profit. Here's to success!

> RIBA Plan of Work glossary

The following presents a glossary of all of the capitalised terms that are used throughout the RIBA Plan of Work 2013. Defining certain terms has been necessary to clarify the intent of a term, to provide additional insight into the purpose of certain terms and to ensure consistency in the interpretation of the RIBA Plan of Work 2013.

'As-constructed' Information
Information produced at the end of a project to represent what has been constructed. This will comprise a mixture of 'as-built' information from specialist subcontractors and the 'final construction issue' from design team members. Clients may also wish to undertake 'as-built' surveys using new surveying technologies to bring a further degree of accuracy to this information.

Building Contract
The contract between the client and the contractor for the construction of the project. In some instances, the Building Contract may contain design duties for specialist subcontractors and/or design team members. On some projects, more than one Building Contract may be required, for example one contract for shell and core works and another for furniture, fitting and equipment (F, F&E) aspects.

Building Information Modelling (BIM)
BIM is widely used as the acronym for 'Building Information Modelling', which is commonly defined (using the Construction Project Information Committee (CPIC) definition) as 'digital representation of physical and functional characteristics of a facility creating a shared knowledge resource for information about it and forming a reliable basis for decisions during its life cycle, from earliest conception to demolition'.

Business Case
The Business Case for a project is the rationale behind the initiation of a new building project. It may consist solely of a reasoned argument. It may contain supporting information, financial appraisals or other background information. It should also highlight initial considerations for the Project Outcomes. In summary, it is a combination of objective and subjective considerations. The Business Case might be prepared in relation to, for example, appraising a number of sites or in relation to assessing a refurbishment against a new-build option.

Change Control Procedures
Procedures for controlling changes to the design and construction following the sign-off of the Stage 2 Concept Design and the Final Project Brief.

Common Standards
Publicly available standards frequently used to define project and design management processes in relation to the briefing, designing, constructing, maintaining, operating and use of a building.

Communication Strategy
The strategy that sets out when the project team will meet, how they will communicate effectively and the protocols for issuing information between the various parties, both informally and at Information Exchanges.

Construction Programme
The period in the Project Programme and the Building Contract for the construction of the project, commencing on the site mobilisation date and ending at Practical Completion.

Construction Strategy
A strategy that considers specific aspects of the design that may affect the buildability or logistics of constructing a project, or may affect health and safety aspects. The Construction Strategy comprises items such as cranage, site access and accommodation locations, reviews of the supply chain and sources of materials, and specific buildability items, such as the choice of frame (steel or concrete) or the installation of larger items of plant. On a smaller project, the strategy may be restricted to the location of site cabins and storage, and the ability to transport materials up an existing staircase.

Contractor's Proposals
Proposals presented by a contractor to the client in response to a tender that includes the Employer's Requirements. The Contractor's Proposals may match the Employer's Requirements, although certain aspects may be varied based on value-engineered solutions, and additional information may be submitted to clarify what is included in the tender. The Contractor's Proposals form an integral component of the Building Contract documentation.

Contractual Tree
A diagram that clarifies the contractual relationship between the client and the parties undertaking the roles required on a project.

Cost Information
The estimate of the construction, or capital, costs for a building, which should be aligned with the Project Budget unless otherwise agreed with the client. Cost Information may also include or be linked to a maintenance cost plan.

Design Programme
A programme setting out the strategic dates in relation to the design process. It is aligned with the Project Programme but is strategic in its nature, due to the iterative nature of the design process, particularly in the early stages.

Design Queries
Queries relating to the design arising from the site, typically managed using a contractor's in-house request for information (RFI) or technical query (TQ) process.

Design Responsibility Matrix
A matrix that sets out who is responsible for designing each aspect of the project and when. This document sets out the extent of any performance specified design. The Design Responsibility Matrix is created at a strategic level at Stage 1 and fine tuned in response to the Concept Design at the end of Stage 2 in order to ensure that there are no design responsibility ambiguities at Stages 3, 4 and 5.

Employer's Requirements
Proposals prepared by design team members. The level of detail will depend on the stage at which the tender is issued to the contractor. The Employer's Requirements may comprise a mixture of prescriptive elements and descriptive elements to allow the contractor a degree of flexibility in determining the Contractor's Proposals.

Feasibility Studies
Studies undertaken on a given site to test the feasibility of the Initial Project Brief on a specific site or in a specific context and to consider how site-wide issues will be addressed.

Feedback

Feedback from the project team, including the end users, following completion of a building.

Final Project Brief

The Initial Project Brief amended so that it is aligned with the Concept Design and any briefing decisions made during Stage 2. (Both the Concept Design and Initial Project Brief are Information Exchanges at the end of Stage 2.)

Handover Strategy

The strategy for handing over a building, including the requirements for phased handovers, commissioning, training of staff or other factors crucial to the successful occupation of a building. On some projects, the Building Services Research and Information Association (BSRIA) Soft Landings process is used as the basis for formulating the strategy and undertaking a Post-occupancy Evaluation (www.bsria. co.uk/services/design/soft-landings/).

Health and Safety Strategy

The strategy covering all aspects of health and safety on the project, outlining legislative requirements as well as other project initiatives, including the Maintenance and Operational Strategy.

Information Exchange

The formal issue of information for review and sign-off by the client at key stages of the project. The project team may also have additional formal Information Exchanges as well as the many informal exchanges that occur during the iterative design process.

Initial Project Brief

The brief prepared following discussions with the client to ascertain the Project Objectives, the client's Business Case and, in certain instances, in response to site Feasibility Studies.

Maintenance and Operational Strategy

The strategy for the maintenance and operation of a building, including details of any specific plant required to replace components.

Post-occupancy Evaluation

Evaluation undertaken post occupancy to determine whether the Project Outcomes, both subjective and objective, set out in the Final Project Brief have been achieved.

Practical Completion

Practical Completion is a contractual term used in the Building Contract to signify the date on which a project is handed over to the client. The date triggers a number of contractual mechanisms.

Project Budget

The client's budget for the project, which may include the construction cost as well as the cost of certain items required post completion and during the project's operational use.

Project Execution Plan

The Project Execution Plan is produced in collaboration between the project lead and lead designer, with contributions from other designers and members of the project team. The Project Execution Plan sets out the processes and protocols to be used to develop the design. It is sometimes referred to as a project quality plan.

Project Information

Information, including models, documents, specifications, schedules and spreadsheets, issued between parties during each stage and in formal Information Exchanges at the end of each stage.

Project Objectives

The client's key objectives as set out in the Initial Project Brief. The document includes, where appropriate, the employer's Business Case, Sustainability Aspirations or other aspects that may influence the preparation of the brief and, in turn, the Concept Design stage. For example, Feasibility Studies may be required in order to test the Initial Project Brief against a given site, allowing certain high-level briefing issues to be considered before design work commences in earnest.

Project Outcomes

The desired outcomes for the project (for example, in the case of a hospital this might be a reduction in recovery times). The outcomes may include operational aspects and a mixture of subjective and objective criteria.

Project Performance

The performance of the project, determined using Feedback, including about the performance of the project team and the performance of the building against the desired Project Outcomes.

Project Programme

The overall period for the briefing, design, construction and post-completion activities of a project.

Project Roles Table

A table that sets out the roles required on a project as well as defining the stages during which those roles are required and the parties responsible for carrying out the roles.

Project Strategies

The strategies developed in parallel with the Concept Design to support the design and, in certain instances, to respond to the Final Project Brief as it is concluded. These strategies typically include:

Acoustic strategy
Fire engineering strategy
Maintenance and Operational Strategy
Sustainability Strategy
Building control strategy
Technology Strategy

These strategies are usually prepared in outline at Stage 2 and in detail at Stage 3, with the recommendations absorbed into the Stage 4 outputs and Information Exchanges.

The strategies are not typically used for construction purposes because they may contain recommendations or information that contradict the drawn information. The intention is that they should be transferred into the various models or drawn information.

Quality Objectives
The objectives that set out the quality aspects of a project. The objectives may comprise both subjective and objective aspects, although subjective aspects may be subject to a design quality indicator (DQI) benchmark review during the Feedback period.

Research and Development
Project-specific research and development responding to the Initial Project Brief or in response to the Concept Design as it is developed.

Risk Assessment
The Risk Assessment considers the various design and other risks on a project and how each risk will be managed, and the party responsible for managing each risk.

Schedule of Services
A list of specific services and tasks to be undertaken by a party involved in the project which is incorporated into their professional services contract.

Site Information
Specific Project Information in the form of specialist surveys or reports relating to the project or site-specific context.

Strategic Brief
The brief prepared to enable the Strategic Definition of the project. Strategic considerations might include considering different sites, whether to extend, refurbish or build new, and the key Project Outcomes as well as initial considerations for the Project Programme and assembling the project team.

Sustainability Aspirations

The client's aspirations for sustainability, which may include additional objectives, measures or specific levels of performance in relation to international standards, as well as details of specific demands in relation to operational or facilities management issues.

The Sustainability Strategy will be prepared in response to the Sustainability Aspirations and will include specific additional items, such as an energy plan and ecology plan and the design life of the building, as appropriate.

Sustainability Strategy

The strategy for delivering the Sustainability Aspirations.

Technology Strategy

The strategy established at the outset of a project that sets out technologies, including Building Information Modelling (BIM) and any supporting processes, and the specific software packages that each member of the project team will use. Any interoperability issues can then be addressed before the design phases commence.

This strategy also considers how information is to be communicated (by email, file transfer protocol (FTP) site or using a managed third-party common data environment) as well as the file formats in which information will be provided. The Project Execution Plan records agreements made.

Work in Progress

Work in Progress is ongoing design work that is issued between designers to facilitate the iterative coordination of each designer's output. Work issued as Work in Progress is signed off by the internal design processes of each designer and is checked and coordinated by the lead designer.

Activities programme

Put reminders into your electronic diary for the following activities. Add others as appropriate to your practice.

Annually
Review SWOT analysis (refer to advice under Stage 0).
Review business plan (refer to advice under Stages 0 and 1).
Review risk management plan (refer to advice under Stage 2).
Review PI cover (refer to advice under Stage 5).
Review core aims and ambitions and amend business plan as necessary.
Review PR material: website, brochures, elevator pitch, etc (refer to advice under Stage 0).
If QA certified, carry out external QA audit.

Six-monthly
Conduct staff personal reviews (refer to advice under Stage 4).
Carry out internal QA audit.

Monthly
Review CRM schedule and update as necessary (refer to advice under Stage 7).
For RIBA Chartered Practices, collate information required for annual RIBA Business Benchmarking (refer to advice under Stage 6).

Weekly
Review Project Programmes (refer to advice under Stage 1).
Review cash flow for projects (refer to advice under Stage 1).
Review cash flow for practice (refer to advice under Stage 1).
Input timesheet data into company spreadsheet or other central record as appropriate (refer to advice under Stage 1).
Read industry journals as appropriate.

Daily
Timesheet for project and non-project activities.
Back up IT system (refer to advice under Stage 3)

Further reading

Bussey, P. (2015) CDM 2015 - *A Practical Guide for Architects and Designers*, London, RIBA Publishing.

Clamp, H., Cox S. and Lupton S. (2012), *Which Contract? 5th edition*, London, RIBA Publishing.

Davies, I. (2014), *Contract Administration: RIBA Plan of Work 2013 Guide*, London, RIBA Publishing.

Evans, H. (2015) *Guide to the Building Regulations (3rd edition)*, London, NBS.

Fairhead, R. (2015), *Information Exchanges: RIBA Plan of Work 2013 Guide*, London, RIBA Publishing.

Finch, R. (2011) *NBS Guide to Tendering: for Construction Projects*, London, RIBA Publishing.

Havard, Dr T. (2008), *Contemporary Property Development, 2nd edition*, London, RIBA Publishing.

Klaschka, R. (2014), *BIM in Small Practices: Illustrated Case Studies*, [London], NBS.

Luder, O. (2012), *Good Practice Guide: Keeping out of Trouble*, London, RIBA Publishing.

Lupton, S. (2011), *Guide to the JCT Intermediate Building Contract IC11*, London, RIBA Publishing.

Lupton, S. (2011), *Guide to the JCT Minor Works Building Contract MW11*, London, RIBA Publishing.

Lupton, S. (2015), *Guide to RIBA Domestic and Concise Building Contracts*, London, RIBA Publishing.

Marks, K. (2016) *HR for Creative Companies*, London, RIBA Publishing

Nutt B. (2009), *Construction Planning Programming and Control, 3rd edition*, Oxford, Wiley-Blackwell.

Ostime, N. (2017) A Commercial Client's Guide to Engaging an Architect, London, RIBA Publishing.

Ostime, N. (2017) A Domestic Client's Guide to Engaging an Architect, London, RIBA Publishing.

Ostime, N. (2013), *RIBA Job Book, 9th edition*, London, RIBA Publishing.

Ostime, N. (2013), *Handbook of Practice Management, 9th edition*, London, RIBA Publishing.

Pelsmakers, S. (2015), *The Environmental Design Pocketbook (2nd edition)*, London, RIBA Publishing.

Phillips, R. (2012), *Good Practice Guide: Fee Management, 2nd edition*, London, RIBA Publishing.

Philips, R. (2012), *A Guide to Letter Contracts*, London, RIBA Publishing.

Phillips, R and RIBA, (2012) *Guide to RIBA Agreements 2010 (2012 Revision)*, London, RIBA Publishing.

Pinder-Ayers, B. (2016) *Financial Management*, London, RIBA Publishing.

Prasad, S. (2014), *Retrofit for Purpose*, London, RIBA Publishing.

Race, S. (2013), *BIM Demystified, 2nd edition*, London, RIBA Publishing.

Reed, R. (2014), *Town Planning: RIBA Plan of Work 2013 Guide*, London, RIBA Publishing.

RIBA, (2013) *A Client's Guide to Engaging an Architect*, London, RIBA Publishing.

Sinclair, D. (2013), *Assembling a Collaborative Project Team*, London, RIBA Publishing.

Sinclair, D. (2013), *Guide to Using the RIBA Plan of Work 2013*, London, RIBA Publishing.

Sinclair, D. (2014), *Design Management: RIBA Plan of Work 2013 Guide*, London, RIBA Publishing.

The Association for Project Safety, (2015) *Principal Designer's Handbook*, London, RIBA Publishing.

Willars, N. (2014), *Project Leadership: RIBA Plan of Work 2013 Guide*, London, RIBA Publishing.

Wevill, J. (2012), *Law in Practice, the RIBA Legal Handbook*, London, RIBA Publishing.

Web resources:

Understanding Risk Management, which can be downloaded from www.architectspi.com/Pages/RiskManagement.aspx.

www.bimtaskgroup.org

www.planningportal.gov.uk.

www.thenbs.com

Index

Index

Index

Index

Image credits

Alistair Nicholls Photography	180–182
And Architects Ltd	152–154
ArchitecturePLB	322–324
Chris Dyson Architects LLP	85, 188, 201–203, 247–249, 270–272
Chris Dyson Architects LLP/Peter Landers	Front cover
Laura Dewe Mathews	229–231
Richard Downer	27–29
Dennis Gilbert / VIEW	140–142
Graticule Architecture	118–120
Jack Hobhouse	55–57
Kneath Associates, after sketches by Nigel Ostime	60
Rachael Smith Photography	170–172
RIBA	14–15, 22, 43, 87, 106, 130, 151, 160, 192, 256, 296
Rural Office for Architecture	308–310
Wai Ming Ng	102, 104
West Architecture	16, 70–72, 213–215
Weston Surman and Deane Architecture	103
Chris Wright	33–35, 126, 289–291.